I WAS A TEENAGE PLAYWRIGHT

I WAS A TEENAGE PLAYWRIGHT

THE FIRST TEN YEARS OF THE SCIROCCO/MAP
MANITOBA HIGH SCHOOL PLAYWRIGHTING COMPETITION

ANGUS KOHM, EDITOR

I Was a Teenage Playwright
first published 2011 by
Scirocco Drama
An imprint of J. Gordon Shillingford Publishing Inc.
© 2011 The Authors

Scirocco Drama Editor: Glenda MacFarlane
Cover design by Terry Gallagher/Doowah Design Inc.
Printed and bound in Canada on 100% post-consumer recycled paper.

We acknowledge the financial support of the Manitoba Arts Council and The Canada
Council for the Arts for our publishing program.

Library and Archives Canada Cataloguing in Publication

I was a teenage playwright: the first ten years of the Scirocco/MAP
High School Playwriting Competition / Angus Kohm, editor.

ISBN 978-1-897289-70-9

1. Canadian drama (English)—21st century. 2. Youths'
writings, Canadian (English). I. Kohm, Angus, 1970–

PS8315.1.I3 2011   C812'.60809283   C2011-907064-2

J. Gordon Shillingford Publishing
P.O. Box 86, RPO Corydon Avenue, Winnipeg, MB Canada R3M 3S3

Acknowledgments

Manitoba Department of Education, Gord Shilllingford, Paula and Owen McKenzie, Stefanie Wiens, Curtis Moore, Zaz Bajon, Steven Schipper, Laurie Lam and The Royal Manitoba Theatre Centre, Veralyn Warkentin, Talia Pura, Kevin Longfield, Patty Hawkins and the University of Winnipeg Theatre Department, Julie Simpson, Gary Jarvis (for directing plays nine out of ten years), and all of our directors (2001-2010): Veralyn Warkentin, Ian Ross, Joff Schmidt, Brenda McLean, Daina Leitold, Chris Sobczak, Demetra Hajidiacos, Daniel Thau-Eleff, Muriel Hogue, Grahame Merke, Maggie Nagle, Nancy Drake, Heather Roberts, Jane Walker, Mike Bell, Eileen Longfield, Elena Anciro, Stefanie Wiens, Heidi Malazdrewich, Alexis Martin, Carolyn Gray, Cory Wojcik, Dan De Jaeger, and Megan Andres; Dramaturges: Jeff Tomson, Bruce McManus, Liesl Lafferty, Ellen Peterson, and Scott Douglas; and everyone else who has helped us over the years. There are way too many of you to list here—but we thank you from the bottom of our hearts.

Table of Contents

Foreword

The Manitoba Association of Playwrights has for more than thirty years been the central organization for playwrights striving to write and produce plays in Manitoba and elsewhere.

Our purpose is to encourage, develop, and workshop, playwrights and their work at all levels, so emphasizing a young playwrights' program is an important, even obvious, goal of MAP.

In the early days, there were various attempts, including workshops, and presentations, of student plays, but it wasn't until the appearance of the Manitoba High School Playwriting Competition, sponsored by Scirocco Drama, that we found the gauge of how to approach the development of young playwrights at its most interesting and lively. The story of how it came about rightly belongs to its originator and present Producer, Angus Kohm, with his introduction to this collection.

Needless to say, it is some sign of success, and importance of the program, that such a collection has been gathered together and published. We hope, however, these plays are for more than a good read or academic reflection. These are plays for use; they work, and would provide a good 'workout' for students, coming from students; or, for that matter, by theatres looking for short, interesting work to present in their season.

What we have discovered in reading hundreds of plays by students who have entered the Competition over the years is that they want to be taken as seriously as more experienced playwrights assume they will be. MAP offers in this competition the opportunity for students to express what cannot be discussed: to use theatre for what is meant to be, a place to unfold life, in all its comic, tragic, and often mixed, bewildering condition.

A sharp fundraising idea, which was the Competition's genesis, has become an important provincial program through diligence and hard work. Angus Kohm has been at the centre of it all, and his voice above all should inform you what has gone on for these now eleven years, and counting. MAP's, and my personal gratitude to him, knows no bounds.

—Rory Runnells

Introduction

The dream began in 1998, when Gary Jarvis and I produced a special one-time fundraiser for MAP; a double bill of new plays called *Mountain Climbing* (by Gary Jarvis) and *The Inner City Dead* (by Angus Kohm). We cast the shows with volunteer actors, most of whom were university or high school students. They were keen and hard working, and when the plays were performed, they drew many friends and family members out to see them—making the fundraiser a huge success.

This got me to thinking... What if we produced a high school playwriting competition? We could pick five high school playwrights, then hire five young, keen recent university graduates to direct them, and then cast a bunch of high school and university students to act in them—and to top it off, we'll have the winners determined by audience vote (so everyone will try to bring out as many supporters as possible)! It seemed like a surefire way to draw big crowds to the show and raise some money to help support MAP.

Surprisingly enough, when I pitched the idea to the MAP Board in 1999 they didn't seem to understand it, and opted instead to authorize a different fundraising project. I had to admit temporary defeat, but I knew that the idea was a good one, so in 2001 I tried again. This time the MAP Board said yes, and the Manitoba High School Playwriting Competition was born.

We didn't really know what we were doing that first year. We sent a call out to high schools, asking for plays, and we got a pretty big response. However, most of the plays were more like TV or movie scripts, with explosions, and car crashes, etc. It seemed as if most high school students didn't know what a play was. We did manage to find five in that huge pile that we felt could work on stage, and in fact were pretty well written. We chose them as our finalists, and went to work. I distributed the scripts to my five hand-picked young directors. We held auditions and actually wound up having to cast every single actor who came out to try for a part (and we were still one actor short). I think having the words "high school" on our audition notices may have deterred some of the older aspiring actors that first year. The directors rehearsed their actors. I encouraged them to get in touch with their playwrights and invite them to rehearsals. Some directors did, other did not. When the opening night of the performances rolled around, we had never actually seen or talked to most of the playwrights. We had to hang a sign at the entrance of the theatre saying, "Playwrights, please identify yourselves", so we didn't accidentally charge them admission to see their own plays. One of our finalists was from Cranberry-Portage, a northern community between The Pas and Flin Flon. We were thrilled when a bus pulled up in front of the theatre delivering her and a large group of supporters from her town. In fact, all of the playwrights showed up (which seemed a little miraculous to us at that time) bringing friends, family, and many students from their schools with them. It seemed as if my idea of having the audience vote to determine the winners was working to convince the playwrights that they had better bring a lot of supporters with them. Needless to say, the event was a huge success. We packed the MTC Warehouse Theatre for two nights, and raised a significant amount of money for MAP.

As I said, I had always believed that this High School Playwriting Competition would be a successful fundraiser, so the fact that it was did not surprise me. What did surprise me, however, was the response that we got from teachers, students, and theatre professionals who came to see the show, or who had been involved in some way in the process. In varying ways, they all said this:

"This High School Playwriting Competition is a great idea. It's an important, valuable and perhaps life-changing opportunity / experience to offer to high school students—some who may want to be writers, others who maybe don't, and in some cases do not think that it's even possible to be writers, actors, artists, etc. We need something like this in Manitoba. You have to do this again."

I think it's fair to say that we were a little stunned by how much people really seemed to love this competition. We had only intended to do it this one time, but we couldn't help but be swayed by all of the encouragement to "do it again" (not to mention the success at the box-office). So, we decided the make the one time fundraiser a two-time fundraiser. But we had learned a few things that first year, so we tried to make a few improvements in the second. Most importantly, we knew that we needed to have better communication with our playwrights. We knew that we had to meet them before the opening night. We also felt that all of the scripts could have benefited from a little re-writing. So, Rory Runnells and I put our heads together and we came up with a plan. We would offer two sessions of dramaturgy to each finalist. The first one would be a meeting between the playwright, and a dramaturge. Being a no-budget affair, it was decided that I would dramaturge three of the five plays, and Jeff Thomson, who was studying dramaturgy at university and volunteering as an assistant dramaturge at MAP's Open Door sessions, would do the other two. Jeff and I met with the students individually and offered them advice on how they might improve their plays. Then the budding playwrights went away for about a month and did some rewrites. We held auditions, and this time we were pleasantly surprised to see more actors than we could possibly cast. It seemed as if word had gotten out about we were doing, and people wanted to be involved. The playwrights were invited to attend the auditions this time, so they could learn firsthand what that process was like, and also so they could have some input as to which actors were cast in their plays. The second set of workshops were held after this, and included directors and actors, as well as the dramaturges and playwrights. The playwrights got to hear their plays read out loud. This was an eye (and ear) opening experience for many of them, who had never heard their words spoken by other people. Everyone offered feedback. Questions were asked. And general first impressions were noted. The playwrights left this workshop with much to think about, and did some more rewriting over the next couple of weeks. Then the plays were rehearsed. Many of the playwrights attended rehearsals, learning what that process was like, and making the occasional adjustment to their lines. By the time the show opened in early June, we did not need to wonder if the playwrights would show up (nor did we need a sign to tell them to identify themselves). This second year was even more successful than the first (both artistically and in terms of attendance). TV stations came out to cover the opening. The newspapers wrote big articles. Everyone was very impressed by what we were doing. And we raised another nice sum of money for MAP.

Once again we were taken aside by many people and told how important this competition was. The playwrights themselves were thrilled by the experience, and were asking about how to continue on with playwriting (and luckily, at that time, we could direct them to the Young Emerging Playwrights Programme—unfortunately, it is no more). Most of all, everyone was telling us, "You have to do this again."

Do it again?! This one-time fundraiser was quickly turning into a major long-term commitment. I was thrilled by the obvious success that we were achieving, but at the same time, it was a lot of work! As Producer, my job started part time in December and got busier and busier until June. And now that we had added these workshops to the process, it was quite a big time commitment for the dramaturges in March and April. Not to mention the directors and actors, many of whom were rehearsing three times a week for six weeks or more.

Everyone had been happy to volunteer his or her time and efforts to a one-time fundraiser. Most had been happy enough to do it a second time, seeing as how the first one was such a big success. But how many times could we do this and not pay the people who were doing the bulk of the work? Where could we get the money to pay people?

Rory and I had another meeting and tried to sort things out. It was becoming clear to us that this playwriting competition could not be a fundraiser for MAP in the long run. It was clearly a valuable thing that was worth doing. It was clearly developing young playwrights. It was clearly raising the profile of MAP, and the work that we do. Clearly, it needed to become a regular programme of MAP… but we just didn't have the budget to do that.

The show must go on, however…so we went ahead with a third year…and a fourth… The work didn't get any easier. In fact, every year we added more aspects to what were doing and worked on improving our system. With each new thing that went wrong, a new rule appeared to prevent the same mistake from happening in the future. We went to new and different directors, not wanting to overtax anyone's goodwill by asking them to volunteer year after year after year. We started to pay very small honorariums to directors, dramaturges, and the producer. Very small honorariums… MAP stopped making money by running this programme, and started thinking about ways to raise money so that we could continue to run it.

Suddenly it was our fifth anniversary, and we held a little celebration at which we made some official announcements. The Manitoba High School Playwriting Competition was definitely going to continue as a permanent programme of MAP. We were naming our top prize after Cora McKenzie, who had won first place two years earlier and then been killed in a tragic car accident. And I, who had created the programme and ran it for five years, would be stepping down. After five years of hard work (for which I had been paid almost nothing), I needed to go back to being a playwright, which believe it or not, gave me a better chance of earning a fair wage for my time (and that's just crazy).

A few months later, Rory called me up and asked me to come back as Producer. He had found some more money, and could offer me a raise. I would still be earning way less than minimum wage, but it was a definite step in the right direction. Maybe it was the months of rest… maybe it was the fact that I already missed doing it… but most likely it was the fact that I truly believed in this programme and didn't want it die out… I agreed to come back.

Over the next five years we grew and improved our programme by leaps and bounds. We began our partnership with Scirocco Drama in our sixth year and have remained happily connected ever since. We've worked with some excellent dramaturges (who are also professional playwrights), such as Bruce McManus, Ellen Peterson and Scott Douglas. Our workshopping process has gotten more involved; the dramaturges are often in frequent contact with the playwrights through e-mail and telephone. We've also added a private Facebook Group where playwrights can discuss their projects with each other, their dramaturges, directors, etc—and where all important dates and information can be posted. We've also been very fortunate to have a resident production stage manager, Julie Simpson, who somehow manages to keep track of all five plays throughout the process, and then runs the whole show during the technical rehearsals and the performances. We couldn't have done it without her (as we learned in year three... okay, we did without her that year, but it's a million times better when she's on the team—and she has been ever since, thankfully).

We've noticed that, in general, the plays being submitted to us have gradually increased in quality over the years. We are receiving far fewer film scripts with explosions and car chases. I would suggest that because of this competition, and the information that we send out to the schools (and the fact that many teachers have encouraged their students to get involved year after year), Manitoba high school students now have a much better understanding of how to write a play! Some finalists come to us having seen our shows in previous years (when their older siblings, or schoolmates, were involved). Many enter the competition more than once, and we have had a few who were finalists two years in a row (or in one case, three). Some playwrights have returned as actors after they graduate. Some have joined MAP and stayed involved in theatre. Others have written fringe shows. When we held a special tenth anniversary party in May of 2010, many former finalists returned to join us in celebrating. Others who couldn't be there (some who are now living as far away as Europe, Toronto, and Washington, D.C.) sent us e-mails congratulating us and reminiscing about the great time they had when they were involved in our programme. In our first ten years, we worked with over 50 high school playwrights, 25 up-and-coming directors, more than 350 volunteer actors, and many other helpers, from musicians, to choreographers, to ushers at the theatre.

One of my biggest regrets is that we didn't keep better track of things (mainly our finalist playwrights) in the very first year of this contest. We only met them briefly at the very end of the process. I tried to track them down to invite them to our tenth anniversary, but could only find one (and he had been a Finalist in the second year, as well). If any of the others are out there, and if they ever see this, I hope they will drop us a line at MAP and let us know how they are doing.

My other big regret is that I can only include ten plays in this collection; one play for each year of our first decade. In some ways, it would have been great to publish every last one of them... but in the end, decisions had to be made. An obvious plan might have been to simply choose the winning play from each year, but that didn't feel right somehow. There has always been some debate, fueled by our system of determining the winners by audience vote, that it isn't always the best play that wins the competition.

"Why not have panels of professionals decide who wins?" some have suggested.

"Because," I tell them, "then we might have winning plays that satisfy some pretentious artists (like me), but fail to connect with the audience." Neither system is perfect. Both are valid. We made our choice when this competition was a one-time fundraiser, and it was, admittedly, motivated by the desire to get as many people out to see the plays as possible.

"But what if one playwright brings two hundred friends and they all vote for his play even though it stinks?"

I guess it could happen...in theory...but in reality it never has. The voting is done by secret ballot, so by and large, most people vote for the play that they like the best (without fear that their sister, son, or best friend will ever know). When you sit in an audience, you can tell when a play is working; when it is connecting with people, drawing them in, entertaining them, moving them, etc. In each of the first ten years of the contest, you could feel which play was going to win. There may have been a couple of close calls, when it was hard to decide which of two were going to come out on top, but there was never a really strange upset based on voting irregularities. And I think that says something about the honesty of an audience that is truly affected by a play.

Having said that, there have been a few plays over the years that were excellent, mature pieces of writing that, for one reason or another, didn't quite make that connection. I have no doubt that a panel of pros would have ranked them higher than the audiences did, and hence we have our controversies.

One or two plays in this collection are examples of this.

Certain themes and issues have come up again and again over the years (young writers share certain obsessions, it would seem). Stylistically we have seen everything from the darkest, most depressing tragedies, to the lightest, funniest comedies. We have seen a few postmodern takes on famous characters and/or people. We have seen stark realism. We have seen satire. We have also seen experiments with form and content. In this collection of ten plays, we have tried to touch on all of these things…but the truth is that we couldn't have done it even if we had included another ten plays. Perhaps, if it sells well, we will get another shot at it…

The biggest thing we miss out on in this collection: a play from the first year. For obvious reasons (mainly the inability to locate most of the playwrights), it just wasn't possible to include one. The first five plays we presented (way back in 2001) are in many ways rougher than all of the subsequent plays, because none of them received any dramaturgical support. But a couple of them stand out in my memory in a way that only the best theatre does.

I think the plays in this collection would stand up next to most of the professionally produced plays I've seen in the past ten years. I hope that each and every one of them finds a new life beyond these pages. Thank you to everyone who has been involved in this programme over the years. And to all of the young, aspiring writers out there… Keep writing plays!

—Angus Kohm

An Ordinary Girl

Lauren Parsons

"This was the first of many plays that we would receive (and in some cases, produce) on the theme of teen suicide; clearly a subject that holds a fascination for many young writers. It won first place in the second year's competition, beating out several other strong plays. None of them, however, connected with—and moved—the audience like this one did." —A.K.

	Blackout. There are five people on stage, standing. Upstage left and right, downstage left and right, And upstage centre. A spotlight on the girl upstage centre is turned on. She has her head down. And she slowly lifts it up.
TAMMY:	Hi. I'm Tammy. This is my life. It's not really much of a story, in my opinion, I'm actually pretty boring. I'm 16, in high school, and have never had a boyfriend. I'm failing math and practically a social outcast. I mean, yes, I do have friends…
	Stage lights up.
STEPHANIE:	Tammy!
ANTHONY:	Hey Tammy!
KELLY:	Hi Tammy!
PAUL:	What's up, Tammy?
	All lights excluding the centre spotlight down.
TAMMY:	Not too many, as you can see. I don't know how well they know me or how well I know them, but they are my friends, I can tell you that. Really… I'd like to be popular, almost more than anything!

Blackout, spotlight on KELLY.

KELLY: Hi, I'm Kelly. Tammy is so fortunate to be best friends with me. I'm popular, gorgeous, smart and completely flawless.

Light on TAMMY.

TAMMY: And she knows it too.

KELLY: It's my job to be there for Tammy, to help her, and to annoy her by complaining about things going wrong in my life, when really I know it's better than hers.

TAMMY: Don't forget stealing all the attention…

KELLY: Did I forget to tell you that I'm great at getting attention? Its almost like all I have to do is snap my fingers and everyone looks at me. Especially the boys. *(She winks.)* Everyone loves me; with a face and personality like this, who couldn't?

Light out on KELLY, Spotlight on TAMMY.

TAMMY: But what about me? So what if I don't have the face, or…the body, or the 'personality'. I must be good for something.

Light on PAUL.

PAUL: Hey Tams, Want to do me a favour?

TAMMY: Oh…right. Favours. The little things in life that help other people get ahead. It's fun to help people, but sometimes it can just be too much… Sure Paul. I'll do you a favour!

PAUL: Great! Can you find out what Kelly thinks of me? I've got my eye on her.

TAMMY: Kelly? Kelly? Of course the guy I'm attracted to is going to want to be with my best friend, right? Its not his fault, Kelly is just a lot better than me. It's not her fault either… It's my fault. I'm not the person I want to be and I don't try hard enough… If only I tried hard enough.

Blackout. Lights up on ANTHONY and STEPHANIE.

ANTHONY: Hey… Steph?… What's up with Tammy lately, she seems… distracted.

STEPHANIE: Oh. I haven't really noticed. She always goes through these little phases. It's OK, really, nothing to worry about… It's just something she always does.

ANTHONY: Well, yeah, but never like this.

Lights out on STEPHANIE.

I haven't known Tammy long. But I've known her long enough to know that something's wrong. I tried to talk to her the other day, but it was like she wasn't even there, her eyes were glazed and there was no expression in her voice. She's so beautiful… I don't think many people actually notice her beauty, especially herself. It's not something that really catches most people's eyes at first glance. You have to get to know her, spend time with her, watch her laugh and get mad…eventually you catch yourself thinking "Wow… This is one of the most beautiful girls in the world".

Lights out on ANTHONY, lights up on TAMMY.

TAMMY: You're beautiful. My mother tells me that every single day. Sometimes, when it's late at night I look in the mirror and see someone else. I see someone who's happy, someone exciting who has confidence. Someone I could never be.

Lights out on TAMMY, lights up on STEPHANIE.

STEPHANIE: I'm scared. I don't know what to be thinking. Do you know what she told me? Do you know what Tammy told me today? She said she has no use for her life and she has been thinking about suicide. I was completely speechless. She must have thought I'm stupid, because I started to cry, right there in front of her. She asked me why I was crying, and I told her, that if she ever killed herself, I'd have to kill myself too. That was a lie, I'd never have the guts to kill myself. I hope Tammy doesn't either. She's my best friend. We met when we were too young to remember, and we've been growing up together since. I don't understand why she's feeling this way.

Lights out on STEPHANIE, lights up on TAMMY.

TAMMY: No one gives a damn about me. Would they care if they never saw me again? Probably not. We're graduating next year and they're all moving away. I'll have no one. I barely have anyone now… I was watching the flame of my candle burn today. I compared it to life, it burns with such a force, such a will…but every flame has its struggle, and with the easiest gust of wind, it blows out. It just feels like it would be easier to blow out.

Lights out on TAMMY, lights up on KELLY and PAUL.

KELLY: Tammy needs to realize she's better than she thinks she is. Looks aren't everything.

PAUL: Tammy needs to realize she's getting nowhere and that popularity and looks are everything.

KELLY: She seems to think she has to be popular to be a better person.

PAUL: Why can't she be more like Kelly?

KELLY: Why can't she act like herself for once? She's always trying to be somebody else. People would appreciate her more if she weren't trying so hard.

PAUL: Did you see her the other day? Sitting alone in the cafeteria? God, sometimes I wonder why I spend my time with such a loser.

KELLY: Sometimes she makes me want to scream "Shut up! you're not a loser!"

                Lights out on KELLY and PAUL, lights up on TAMMY.

TAMMY: There are times that I wonder what people see in me. Why they're still around. All I ever do lately is complain about life and how much it sucks. How do I change that? Maybe I'm not supposed to change that... Maybe it's fate. There's fate to everything...to the reason why we're living here, to falling in love. Every small thing we do, there's always a bigger reason behind it all.

                Lights up on ANTHONY.

ANTHONY: If I said I loved you, what would you do? Would you believe me? Would you say you loved me too? I'm going to tell her how I feel. I'm going to. I'm going to. I can't. I'm too shy. I could never tell her... Well, maybe tomorrow.

                Lights up on PAUL, KELLY, and STEPHANIE.

PAUL, KELLY,
STEPH: Anthony and Tammy, sitting in a tree...

ANTHONY: Maybe not tomorrow...eventually...

PAUL, KELLY,
STEPH: K-I-S-S-I-N-G...

ANTHONY: But...what would our friends think?

PAUL, KELLY,
STEPH: First comes love, Then comes marriage, then comes the baby in the baby carriage!

ANTHONY: Would you shut up! Damnit. No. I can't tell her, its too embarrassing.

                Lights out on ANTHONY, KELLY, STEPHANIE, PAUL.

TAMMY: I can't take it anymore! People are expecting too much out of me. They want me to be myself, they want me to be like my sister, they want me to be like Kelly, they want me to be different. I can't be different. I don't want to be, I want to be myself. And even being myself isn't good enough for me. I don't deserve anything in my life, I don't want my life anymore. When I push, they push harder…there's no use in trying anymore… No use at all…goodbye.

STEPHANIE: *(V.O.)* Tammy…don't do anything stupid… I love you too much.

TAMMY: Liar…

PAUL: *(V.O.)* You can't do this…we're buddies, remember?

TAMMY: Another lie…

KELLY: *(V.O.)* Oh come on Tammy, life isn't that bad!

TAMMY: Like you know…you're full of lies…

ANTHONY: *(V.O.)* I think I love you, Tammy…

TAMMY: LIARS!! All of you!! Just Go Away!! Go away… Leave me alone!! No more… Goodbye!!

ANTHONY: *(V.O.)* TAAAAAAMMMYYYYY!!!!!!!

                Blackout. You hear TAMMY's body fall to the ground, a few moments of silence, lights up on STEPHANIE.

STEPHANIE: Tammy killed herself last week. On a Friday, after school. I was the first person her family called.

                Lights up, all except TAMMY are standing where they were.

PAUL: Tammy… she wouldn't have done this if I didn't tease her all the time…

KELLY: No. It's because she felt like a second next to me. As if everyone looked right through her, and saw me…

ANTHONY: No. It was because she never knew how I felt... All she ever wanted was someone to love her.

Lights out on all, except STEPHANIE.

STEPHANIE: Would she have killed herself, if she knew how much we cared? If we had spent a little extra time each day, to express our feelings? If we had tried harder to know what we could do to make things better? If we had done something... would she still be alive today?

Lights up on everyone.

KELLY: I'll miss you Tammy. I'm sorry. When you were acting so shy, I should have helped you to be more outgoing.

PAUL: I should have defended you, when other people were making fun of you, instead of going along with it like I didn't care.

STEPHANIE: I should have told you, that you used to be my best friend.

ANTHONY: I should have known that if you have something to say that could make a difference, you shouldn't wait, because you never know what will happen tomorrow. You might just lose your chance. I love you.

The End.

On the Road

Colin Shelton

"This play took third place in our second year. It was a unique and challenging script that many people admired. Interestingly enough, Colin was not only beaten by Lauren, but also by his own cousin who took second place with a romantic period drama set during the war years. It would have been nice to include all three plays for your perusal, but we've still got eight years left to get through..." —A.K

Samuel Beckett ....an old man

Judith Shakespeare ....a woman in Elizabethan dress

James Joyce ....a man with an eyepatch

> *Dingy light, as of a single, uncovered lightbulb. BECKETT sits at center stage with knees bent, hands resting on knees.*

BECKETT: *(Stares at audience for an uncomfortably long period before speaking.)* Nothing to be done. I thought you were gone for ever, but here you are. I will call you Basil. You certainly seem like a Basil.

> *Enter JOYCE. He moves across the stage slowly, circling BECKETT.*

(While JOYCE is walking.) I suppose there remains only this. You are Basil, and I have been here much too long. How long have I been here? Weeks, days, seconds, always.

JOYCE: *(Aside.)* Days.

BECKETT: *(Dryly.)* Always. I don't remember ever coming to this place, and so I must have always been here. For that matter, I don't remember Basil ever arriving so he must also have always been here.

Enter JUDITH SHAKESPEARE. She stares quizzically at the bizarre scene on the stage.

So as I have always been here, and Basil has always been here, one could say I have always been with Basil, or that Basil and I have always been together. And as Basil and I have always been together, Basil ought to know me fairly well, and I ought to know Basil. And if we know each other really well, then perhaps there is a reason he and I are both here.

SHAKESP: *(To BECKETT.)* Sir?

BECKETT: The only problem then is that I ought to be frightfully bored by his company, if we have always been together. I might know every one of his thoughts by now. I might know the reasons he does the things he does. And he the same of me.

SHAKESP: Sir?

BECKETT: The reason he and I are both here, might be to become frightfully bored of one another, so to speak. But that is if there is any reason at all. And is it at all reasonable that I should have been here forever? And yet I have been here forever. There is no one here to deny it.

JOYCE: Not at all!

SHAKESP: *(Getting angry.)* Sir!

BECKETT: That is not to say that there is no one here at all. Obviously I am here, and Basil is here or else there would be no one for me to be frightfully bored of. But who told me Basil's name was Basil? I don't remember Basil's voice. Oh well, voices aren't that important. After all, some people have no voices at all, and still say a great deal. But that does not tell me who told me Basil's name. Was it Basil or somebody else? And if it was somebody else, where are they now? Or are they still here, always? Always coming back to that? Well, perhaps there's nothing for it.

SHAKESP: *(Runs up to JOYCE. Speaks angrily.)* Sir! Pray tell, why will he not answer me?

JOYCE: *(Stops walking. Speaks, but not quite to JUDITH.)* Some men aren't interested in answers, only questions.

SHAKESP: Sir, as I am neither man nor interested in ceaseless questions, I implore you give me help. *(JOYCE resumes his walking, at a quicker pace.)* I am making for the great city of London, but my road has lost herself amongst the rest, and none of them has offered to show me the way back to her.

JOYCE: I have heard it said that when one tires of London, one tires of life itself.

SHAKESP: Good Sir, I know aught of they city except that it is the one place where I may fulfill my desire, satisfy my passions. Thou must know I am at heart a plain dealing playwright. If I had my mouth I would sing out to the muses! I hear the whisperings of Euterpe, and I cannot but follow them where they lead.

JOYCE: And so to Oo...Oot...Ootarp?

SHAKESP: No, Sir, to London!

   JOYCE trips over BECKETT.

BECKETT: What is this? Some trick of the light, or perhaps a machination of Basil's...get up, and begone! I no longer need such foolishness!

SHAKESP: *(Stomps over to help JOYCE up. Speaks angrily to BECKETT.)* I say, Sir, you are a most cruel and inhospitable madman. It seems to me you know but strange pleasures! You abuse your sole accomplice! *(To JOYCE, as BECKETT gets to his feet.)* My thrice spoken hail fell bluntly on your ears, while your strange companion at least would hear me speak.

BECKETT: And did he please you?

SHAKESP: Whether he pleased me or no you have not! *(Turns to JOYCE.)* Sir, you need not heed his words, though if you will help me, I shall soon be gone. Which way to London?

BECKETT: And whence from London?

SHAKESP: Nowhere, I hope! This journey hath been arduous enough.

BECKETT: So to London, to sit with swarms of itinerant Dubliners, and lament the prosperity so nearly groped.

SHAKESP: I go not there sir.

BECKETT: Oh?

SHAKESP: My destination is a place of vigour where everyday the masses marvel, as men don new robes, and new airs, and so let the day dawn anew on a different land...where the fantastic can leap, and bound, whirl, and meddle with the mundane! I go to no place where life is tossed aside, but rather to the place where she is made beautiful and bizarre!

BECKETT: And what am I, then? *(Before SHAKESPEARE can reply.)* Come, have you seen 'the fantastic' bounding about? Strange that words spoken so emphatically should mean so little... *(Aside.)* What does it matter anyway? This is all completely irrational as it is... *(Turning as if looking for something.)* Perhaps the *(SHAKESPEARE starts walking toward the back of the stage.)* My God, girl, where are you going?

SHAKESP: To London.

BECKETT: Without knowing the way? I suppose that is how most people get anywhere. You, girl, come sit; don't act like a drunkard stumbling about with only some vague idea of where she's going.

SHAKESP: Sir, the way is clear to me, in that I must not tarry here. Nay, I may not know the road, but the lost and lonely pilgrim's path profits the walker more than anything the waiter.

BECKETT: Waiting for what, girl? Come hither, and we'll wait for
                this together.

JOYCE: Or apart.

SHAKESP: Know you the way to London?

JOYCE: But a little.

BECKETT: Why to London? I thought we were to wait.

SHAKESP: (Exasperated.) Nay sir! You might wait. I will live a
                wanderer ere I sit in idyll on the road.

BECKETT: (To audience.) I see we will get nowhere with this line
                of inquiry.

JOYCE: Reasoning.

SHAKESP: Sir, you will get nowhere. I will get away.

BECKETT: Then tell me finally where 'away' is. Plainly, where are
                you going?

SHAKESP: (Frustrated.) Had you but listened to a single pretty
                word of mine, that you could have heard. Good day,
                sir (Exits.)

JOYCE: Good day, sir. (Stands behind BECKETT.)

BECKETT: So it is. Again I am alone without frivolities. No more
                plot, no more silly characters. I am alone. (Begins
                pacing. JOYCE follows him.) Only my thoughts fill this
                place. Is it my place? It might as well be. Without me,
                there is no one here. Without me there is nothing.
                (Stops. Looks at his hand.) Or am I? I have forgotten
                Basil. Where is he?

                        Runs about stage, looking this way and that. JOYCE
                        directly behind him at all times. Suddenly stops, turns,
                        and faces JOYCE.

                (Angrily, pointing to the wings.) Out! Out! I cannot
                stand it any longer. This place is mine. I am this place.
                There can be no intrusions!

JOYCE runs for side of stage, but runs right into JUDITH SHAKESPEARE as she re-enters. They fall over.

SHAKESP: Saint Swithun! What alarum sounds?

JOYCE: Nothing.

BECKETT: Basil. This is Basil's work. *(Walks over to SHAKE-SPEARE and JOYCE, still lying on a heap on the floor. To SHAKESPEARE.)* Who are you?

SHAKESP: My name is Judith Shakespeare, lover, fighter, learne—

BECKETT: Yes, yes, and who sent you?

SHAKESP: None but the graces, sir.

BECKETT: No! It was Basil.

SHAKESP: Sir I know not of whom you speak. Given time I might know him better.

BECKETT: *(Turns away from the two on the floor.)* Why? Oh, why?

SHAKESP: *(Stands.)* Sir! Of what speaketh you? Is Basil some great beast of a man, an enemy of yours? Is Basil a petty sneak, who has stolen your purse, *(Aside)* Though I think it more likely someone'd steal his roof.

BECKETT: *(Suddenly changed.)* Perhaps she will know. *(Faces SHAKESPEARE directly.)* Listen, girl. You can hear him watching. He and I have been here always. Sometimes I have had to watch him, but he is always watching me. I cannot think without him watching.

SHAKESP: Sir, speak plainly!

BECKETT: I have been sitting here forever, wondering what might happen next. And now I see it. Basil is lethargic. He keeps looking back to me, hoping I will be something he has not seen. And indeed I am. I show him much. My thoughts make him cringe, and weep, and laugh. I am always something more, filling this place with something more.

SHAKESP: Sir, what kind of man are you? What manner? Your speech is distressed, your words… What sayest thou that I might not hear? What is the, the…

JOYCE: Reason.

SHAKESP: Why tell you me this?

BECKETT: Girl, do you not listen?

SHAKESP: I day say sir, my position is safe upon that field.

BECKETT: And it still isn't clear.

SHAKESP: Sir, I cannot stand this idle chatter. Tell me what you mean!

BECKETT: I mean nothing. My meaning is gone.

JOYCE: Entirely.

SHAKESP: *(Stands silently perplexed for a time.)* Where has your meaning gone?

BECKETT: To him.

SHAKESP: To whom?

JOYCE: Basil.

BECKETT: Oh, what does it matter. You already know. *(Turns away.)* She wouldn't have come if she didn't know. No one ever arrives without knowing something of the plot. It is all illusion, poor players---

SHAKESP: *(Groans in frustration.)* Enough of that! Thou willst not show me the way to leave? Then I will show myself. Thou willst know it was not on my account I returned here. Thou art the bane of my intellect, moaning oh woe on Basil, Basil, Basil.

BECKETT: I know where you want to go.

SHAKESP: Good. I've said it often enough. Goodbye sir!

BECKETT: *(Grabs SHAKESPEARE to stop her leaving. Becomes grave suddenly.)* No. You have not walked the road before, and I know all too much of it.

SHAKESP: *(Hushed.)* Then tell me finally what thou wantest.

BECKETT: I? I want to know. I want to explain and—

SHAKESP: Sir, you've spoken your soliloquy.

BECKETT: *(To no one.)* Yes, now is the time for a chorus. *(To SHAKESPEARE.)* Sit.

JOYCE: What?

> BECKETT releases SHAKESPEARE, and motions toward center stage with his head. She peers at him in hesitation, then steps boldly to center stage and sits. BECKETT begins to pace, possibly in a circular fashion.

BECKETT: Girl, you are going to London. We know this because you say you that you are, and though we don't really know, we are not going to doubt you. That leaves many questions. Will you be going there if you never arrive? But the most important is: where are you coming from?

SHAKESP: Well, I—

BECKETT: Nay! I slip in my age. The most important question is: have you written anything?

SHAKESP: Indeed, that I have done. Sir, I can answer your question most resoundingly.

BECKETT: Well, what have you written? Out with it! What sonnet has thy pen tickled?

SHAKESP: It is an epic.

BECKETT: Oh, dear. That's just the sort of thing he wants isn't it.

SHAKESP: It is a fine epic! If your muttering slanders it, your tongue will be mine.

BECKETT: None of that please, Miss Shakespeare. What is the piece's name?

SHAKESP: "The Town" it is called.

JOYCE: All ours.

BECKETT: And it is going to the city. Well, I must see it.

SHAKESP: And who, pray, art thou to see such a thing?

BECKETT: *(Scoffs.)* Who am I? What a question to ask… *(Glares at audience.)* One would think the answer apparent to old acquaintances. *(Turns back to SHAKESPEARE.)* You might call me Samuel, and my demands are most appropriate in this place.

SHAKESP: *(Rolls eyes.)* Then here it is. *(Produces crumpled manuscript from pocket.)* Take it.

BECKETT: *(Flipping through the pages.)* A bold dramatis personae. You propose to have fifty actors on the stage?

SHAKESP: With good reason, sir! The town does not exist without inhabitants.

BECKETT: No, each place must have its characters. What clever words he wants from me!

SHAKESP: The crowd enters page the third.

BECKETT: Indeed…"I marked it like the countenance of one by death undone."

SHAKESP: You make that sound ghastly. Give it to me.

             She stretches out her arm, to take the manuscript from BECKETT. Then, before taking it, she retracts her hand.

             Nay, I need it not! My own words ought to fill my soul if already improving paper. The lover speaks:

"I marked it like the countenance of one by death undone, and idling in despair, my dream—", no, it will not do. Sir Samuel return to the twenty-seventh leaf, and read the lover's speech, I'll speak the lady's part.

BECKETT: *(Skeptically.)* Indeed. *(Pacing as he reads.)* "I marked it like the countenance of one by death undone, and idling in despair, my dream of living on with music gone. 'Twas like my dream was creased by folds of care, as faces with eyes sunken, changed by grief. And as I kept on dreaming without note, without the sound of any falling leaf, my own most sacred words died in my throat."

SHAKESP: *(Taking a step towards BECKETT.)* "Then I am glad thy thoughts were but mere dreams, that need not change our living course at all. Yet sleeping sometimes proves more than it seems, and dreaming might foretell a final fall. Now let us fall 'fore Cupid and embrace, and no more worries shall bescar thy face." Now enter the merry Baker, oh but who shall speak his part… *(Beckons to JOYCE.)* Sir, wouldst thou join us in our reading?

JOYCE: *(Reading over BECKETT's shoulder.)* "Why, what behold I here if not true love? A terrible mistake I'd make if not. I'll hide me in the tree and sit above these gentle doves who recently but fought."

BECKETT: Now enter Father Bartholomew.

SHAKESP: Oh! And who shall speak his part? I shall, for 'tis a grand speech explaining all the rest.

BECKETT: But the Lady Cynthia speaks immediately after Bartholomew.

SHAKESP: 'Tis no matter.

BECKETT: No, it's nothing.

JOYCE: Nothing at all!

SHAKESP: *(Deepens her voice, to begin the speech of Father Bartholomew.)* "It has been so long since I began my quest," *(Meanwhile, BECKETT has flipped ahead several pages in the manuscript and is reading intently. SHAKESPEARE takes notice and stops reciting.)* Fie! You pay no attention. How dare you quote my lines and then not heed them!

BECKETT: Lines as in the third act: "I took it down and learned it all by rote, as surely as if I had been a goat?"

SHAKESP: 'Tis from scripture! The goat is the goat of atonement being led—

BECKETT: *(Turns to JOYCE.)* And what of this: look in the following scene, not two lines after she had been declared dead, the Lady Cynthia begins to speak again.

SHAKESP: In spectral form of course! Her ghost rises up from the corpse and speaks the name of her killer, "Is this the dagger that launched a—"

BECKETT: You've not thought this through.

SHAKESP: I have! 'Tis my finest, to set upon the London stage.

JOYCE: And not all there is finery.

BECKETT: You need London more than it needs you.

SHAKESP: *(Angrily steps toward BECKETT.)* What is your meaning?

BECKETT: *(Waving the manuscript.)* This needs improving. *(Sarcastically.)* Had I twenty minutes, I could not sing all the praises of this play.

SHAKESP: You understand it not.

BECKETT: That's just it! Your mixed metaphors are confusing, not enlightening. Half your rhymes are merely comical, and your stage directions are impractical.

These things would be obvious if the piece were produced.

SHAKESP: *(Steps back from BECKETT, towards center stage.)* I see your meaning. Then what way to London, Sam? I could not bear to live apart from perfection. If the road to London be the way required, 'tis the way I choose to tread. Though my 'Town" might dwindle to a hamlet, the lesser crowd might wrestle the piece into brilliance.

BECKETT: *(To no one.)* And in your brilliance is... *(To SHAKESPEARE.)* Girl, goodbye.

SHAKESP: But Sam, we've but begun! You have some learning in such matters, teach me how to change my play. We could walk the road together—

JOYCE: And who knows the road better than the pilgrim?

BECKETT: You are beyond my teaching. I've said all I need to say.

SHAKESP: Then that is still not all I need to hear. Samuel, you cannot treat me this way. You cannot criticize my work, and leave me stranded. I'll accept 'tis not perfect, but I cannot let it stay that way. I'm sure you can help me, teach me how to write it better.

BECKETT: No, I doubt even I could do that. *(Turns to leave.)*

SHAKESP: But Sam, is there no truth in the work?

BECKETT: Oh, aye. Truth enough for Basil.

JOYCE: Of course!

SHAKESP: Not Basil!

BECKETT: Yea, Basil! Let him watch you. Adieu, Miss Shakespeare! *(Exit BECKETT.)*

> *While SHAKESPEARE watches BECKETT leave, exit JOYCE stealthily to the other side.*

SHAKESP: *(Calling after BECKETT.)* Sir Samuel! *(Turns to audience.)* No help from him. And still no road to London. No way— Oh, fie! *(Falls into sitting position at center stage.)* I am alone, with but an ill-shaped manuscript, and watching Basil. "Tis nothing...nothing to be done... but writing.

        The End.

.COM

Cora McKenzie

"This is a very special play for us. It was a clever, cutting edge, crowd-pleasing comedy that easily won first place in our third year. Cora was an extremely talented young writer who almost certainly would have continued writing with much success, had she not been the victim of a tragic accident. We named the top prize after her in our fifth anniversary year." —A.K.

> *GIRL enters left, strides with head up and goes down right while GUY enters right. He walks quickly looking around him very self-conscious of where he is. Before sitting , both see each other. The guy kind of half smiles then looks away and down. She gives him a quizzical look and then makes a quiet snort and looks him up and down critically yet confidently. They continue down to computers and sit.*

GIRL: *(Types while thinking aloud confidently.)* OK…www. yahoo/chatcanada.com.

GUY: *(Types while thinking aloud.)* Ummm OK ummm…oh, right, yahoo! OK chat..teen. Name..there..wow this chat is almost empty.

GIRL: *(Thinks aloud.)* Only one person in here…HUNK 123, OK. *(Starts to type.)* Hello HUNK 123.

> *Both characters type with each line, unless otherwise indicated, as they 'talk' to each other.*

HUNK 123: Hello, ICE CAT.

ICE CAT: How are you?

HUNK: Good and you?

ICE CAT: Good, asl?

HUNK: What?

ICE CAT: Age/sex/location.

HUNK: Oh, OK... 34 male Canada.

ICE CAT: I'm 33, female, and Canadian.

HUNK: Cool!

ICE CAT: Stats?

HUNK: Huh?

ICE CAT: You're new at this aren't you?

HUNK: Yeah, sorry.

ICE CAT: That's OK. Stats means what do you look like.

HUNK: Oh, OK, ummm, I'm 6'5", 220 lbs. have brown hair and brown eyes.

ICE CAT: *(Thinks out loud.)* Wow, he's hot. *(Types.)* Sounds cool, I'm 6' 0", 120 lbs have blonde hair and blue eyes.

HUNK: You sound pretty.

ICE CAT: *(Thinks.)* I'm not. *(Types.)* ty.

HUNK: Huh?

ICE CAT: Thank you.

HUNK: So where are you in Canada.

ICE CAT: Manitoba and u?

HUNK: Hey, me too. I'm from Winnipeg.

ICE CAT: Hey, me too.

HUNK: Maybe we should meet sometime.

ICE CAT: *(Thinks.)* Yeah, right, like he would want to meet a dork like me. *(Types.)* Yeah, sure that would be cool.

HUNK: So what do u do?

ICE CAT: I'm a model.

HUNK: *(Thinks.)* Whoa, she must really be hot. *(Types.)* That's so cool. *(Thinks a moment, then types.)* I'm a brain surgeon.

ICE CAT: *(Thinks.)* Jackpot! *(Types.)* Oh, OK.

HUNK: *(Tries to type. Then says out loud.)* What the hell?

Oh, man, this stupid thing is frozen! *(Starts to bang on computer and desk.)*

ICE CAT: So what are your interests?

HUNK: *(Continues to bang computer while making angry mutterings.)*

ICE CAT: *(Looks over at HUNK.)* Uh, this is a library not a hockey rink and besides the 'hit it harder till it works' idea doesn't really apply to computers. *(Types, irritated.)* Hello? Are you there?

HUNK: *(Stands up and unplugs computer with an angry yank and a glare at ICE CAT; then he plugs it back in, sits back down and glares at the computer.)*

ICE CAT: *(Getting annoyed.)* Helllllllllooooooo!!!!!

HUNK: *(Thinks.)* Jeez, I hope she didn't log off! *(Types.)* Yahoo, teen, chat…

ICE CAT: Fine, I'm leaving, goodbye. *(ICE CAT stands up and starts to gather up backpack.)*

HUNK: Hey, hey, I'm back, sorry my computer froze.

ICE CAT: *(Sees screen and sits back down.)* Oh, that's OK. *(Thinks.)* Phew!

HUNK: Thanks. *(Thinks.)* Phew.

ICE CAT: So what are your interests?

HUNK: I like football, baseball, hockey and soccer. You?

ICE CAT: Ummm…me too.

HUNK: Really? Did you catch the Blue Bombers game last
                night?

ICE CAT: *(Thinks.)* Oh, crap. *(Types.)* Uh, yeah, it was…intense…

HUNK: Yeah, I know we might actually get into the playoffs
                this year!

ICE CAT: .   Yeah, that would be cool.

HUNK: That would be sweet!

ICE CAT: Yeah, and maybe we could win the Stanley Cup!

HUNK: Stanley? Don't you mean the Grey Cup?

ICE CAT: *(Thinks.)* Shoot. *(Types.)* Oh, yeah, sorry. Blonde
                moment. *(Thinks.)* Oh, great, that was dumb.

HUNK: Yeah… so which magazines do you model for?

ICE CAT: Victoria's Secret.

HUNK: *(Aloud.)* YES!

ICE CAT: *(Looks over divider, says to HUNK.)* Shh! *(Types.)* Which
                hospital do you work at?

HUNK: Um, the big one.

ICE CAT: *(Skeptical.)* Big one.

HUNK: *(Thinks.)* Oh, shoot, which one is that? *(Types.)* You
                know that big one downtown.

ICE CAT: You mean Health Sciences?

HUNK: Yeah, that one.

ICE CAT: Oh, OK. *(Looks questionably at the computer.)*

HUNK: So do you have a boyfriend?

ICE CAT: *(Laughs, thinks.)* Yeah, right. *(Types.)* No, do you have a girlfriend?

HUNK: *(Thinks.)* Sweet! What are the chances? A single lingerie model! Man, too bad I wasn't ten years older.

(Types.) No, do you want one?

ICE CAT: Sure.

HUNK: Cool. We should go to a party sometime.

ICE CAT: *(Enthusiastic.)* Yeah, that would be great!

HUNK: Yeah, it could be. If it doesn't get too heavy, if you know what I mean.

ICE CAT: *(Unsure.)* Ummm, yeah. *(Thinks.)* But isn't that the point of parties.

HUNK: I mean the last one I went to, jeez, it's like, for them all the only point in life is to get wasted. They don't care about anything except having fun and getting away, getting far away. I want to do that too…get far away from here—but not like that, I mean for real, not just a stolen moment.

ICE CAT: Yeah, I guess it can be shallow but it could be, I mean, it CAN be fun sometimes. *(Thinks.)* If only I was given the chance. If only they'd take one second out of their self-involved lives and realize there are other people here too. Not just them. And we have feelings too.

Lights go down except on ICE CAT.

I want to be one of them but they won't allow it. I'm too smart or too weird. One of them look at me or even like me? How dare I conceive of such a horrible thing? How dare I even have stupid feelings for one of them? How dare I not hide those feelings? I mean I thought I was hiding them but I guess I'm not that great of an actress. And it seemed innocent enough just asking Mark to come over to my house to finish the team banners, I mean we're both on the spirit committee. But oh, no he had to give me that look, that look that says, "And who the hell are you? Do you even exist? And where do you get the nerve to try to hang out with me? God, you are so pathetic, just go away, I don't want to have to deal with a little Bug like you."

And it could've ended there. He could have just walked away and I would've been put back in my place, and seen the truth, but oh, no, his good buddy Dean had to say, no, bellow, "Ho, ho, looks like some one has the hots for you Mark. It must be your lucky day." And Mark had to grumble "it is not". Just loud enough for me to hear and THEN he walked away, with EVERYONE knowing the truth, about my stupid feelings for a disgusted boy. I just stood there like a naked idiot. And now I have to sit across from another witness of that travesty, in my place, where I 'BELONG'. Where at least, I guess, I don't have to be the weird one. And now for some reason they're coming in here too. Well they can't take everything away from me. They can embarrass me, they can force me to stand on the outside looking in. But they will never make me feel strange here—where I belong. They will never make me desert that, desert me, even if I am pathetic. A pathetic girl with emotions and instincts, who's just like them *(Pauses.)* But they don't see that. *(Lights back up.) (Types)* They exclude me without even tryin' to get to know me. They judge me from afar and don't even care who I am.

HUNK: Who? The other models?

ICE CAT: Yeah.

HUNK: That sucks. Well, if I were there I'd fight them for you.

ICE CAT: They're models. I'm not sure how much of a fight they could put up, lol.

HUNK: Lol?

ICE CAT:	Laugh out loud. *(Starts to hit the tower.)* Come on, come on. *(Hits it again.)*
HUNK:	*(To ICE CAT.)* Hey, easy there, hitting it harder won't make it work better you know.
ICE CAT:	Oh, shut up! *(Thinks.)* I hope he didn't leave, oh, finally! *(Typing.)* Hi, again, this stupid piece of crap froze for a second! Now what were we talking about?
HUNK:	Umm, work I think.
ICE CAT:	I hate working at MacDonald's. Yuck!!
HUNK:	MacDonald's? Why does MacDonald's need a model?
ICE CAT:	*(Thinks.)* Oops! *(Types.)* Oh, umm. I'm gonna be in the next commercial for them,
HUNK:	*(Thinks.)* Awesome, my girlfriend on TV! *(Types.)* Oh, really? Cool! I'll have to watch out for it.
ICE CAT:	Oh, it's not on TV here, just, ummmm, in Europe.
HUNK:	Oh, that's OK. I have a satellite feed. Do you know which station?
ICE CAT:	*(Thinks.)* Yikes! Uhh… *(Types.)* Umm, it's in French.
HUNK:	You know French?
ICE CAT:	Uh, me oui.
HUNK:	Oh, cool. So do I. Combien du anne est-ce que vous etudiez Francais?
ICE CAT:	*(Thinks.)* Oh, no. Now what…ummm. *(Types.)* Actually I know only France French, they're different.
HUNK:	Oh, OK.
ICE CAT:	*(Thinks.)* Phew. *(Types.)* So do you
HUNK:	Oh, yeah, I have a brother, he's where he is.

ICE CAT: Really ? What happened?

HUNK: Well, it all happened when I was 16, and he was 18, and he wanted to go to Hollywood and be an actor…

                (Lights dim on all except HUNK.) And my dad was like 'that won't feed your family, it's not a good enough job to put food on the table" and my brother was all like "Well, I don't have a family, and I only have to fend for myself" And my Dad started getting mad "oh, that's really mature, what if you get sick, what if your mother or I get sick. How could you pay the bills?" And now they started to scream, I mean really getting into it. "Why do I have to be mature for everyone? Can't I live my own life or at least try?" "Because that's what being a man is! Being mature and looking after your family!" "No, that's what a family man is, not me, why can't you look after mom when she gets sick?" "I can look after her, but one should always have a back up plan!" "Oh, is that all I am to you? A back up plan, a convenient person to get out of trouble? Is that all you had me for?" "Of course not! But this is a duty of the first son!" And that just ticked my brother off more. "I didn't choose to be the first son! I don't want this duty!" "Well, you don't get choices in life. You have to be responsible for your family." "Yeah, and then have no life of my own! I don't want to do it that way!!!"

                "Well, that's the way of the world." "No, your world, dad, not mine!" And then Troy picked up his suitcase, he kissed mom on the cheek and then said to me , "Be thankful you are the second son, Brad, maybe then you can have a life." *(Types.)* And then he walked out just like that and Dad didn't even try to stop him, I mean isn't he supposed too? I mean can't he accept Troy as he is? At least Troy's brave enough to show his true face. I don't hide. I just am so afraid of not being in the 'box' . I act like who I should be. A good son. A good friend. Who doesn't think. Who doesn't care. Nothing is supposed to matter just to be cool. They don't see the truth. Not even my dad. He doesn't see what's important. He let Troy go...just leave and walk out of our lives, maybe forever.

Long pause.

ICE CAT: *(Thinks.)* Wow. *(Types.)* I am so sorry HUNK. *(Pause.)* You know I always saw the 'box" as my...goal. I always wanted to be cool.

HUNK: It's not, we're not. At least out where you are there is truth and you can see it and say it.

ICE CAT: Yeah, I guess no one hears it or sees me but at least I do know my true self. *(Both look away from computers and look around room until their eyes meet. HUNK bangs computer.)*

             (Says.) What are you doing here anyway? The sports section's over there.

HUNK: *(Says.)* Hey, this is a free country.

ICE CAT: Not that you would know anything about our constitution.

HUNK: Well, at least I'm not stuck on one of these things everyday.

ICE CAT: I'm not stuck! I choose to be here... But seriously do you even know where the power button is on that thing?

HUNK: I figured it out.

ICE CAT: Yeah, I heard the way you figured it out.

HUNK: Yeah, I just followed your example!

ICE CAT: *(Scowls.)* Isn't there a pep rally somewhere you should be attending?

HUNK: What? And leave you here all alone with these 10 pound paperweights?

ICE CAT: Don't mock computers. Their technology is so much more advanced than you could ever grasp. So just go back to your drinking buddies and climb back into your own ignorant 'box'.

HUNK: *(Looks at her strangely for a second.)* Right after the library closes.

ICE CAT: *(Moans and roll eyes.) (Types.)* Hey, sorry, I left you there for a second. Jeez, some guys…They can be such jerks.

Glares over at HUNK and shakes head.

HUNK: Well, some girls can be pretty big pains too!

ICE CAT: Some people though, they don't respect anything! They just take the world as it is and don't appreciate it for its wonders. Like, really, they're not even interested in how it all works.

HUNK: I know. But you can't tell or show people you're interested. Oh, no, that would not be cool!

ICE CAT: But I'm sure you have lots of intelligent people surrounding you at H.S.C.

HUNK: Where?

ICE CAT: Your hospital.

HUNK: *(Thinks.)* Oh, right, shoot… *(Types.)* Oh, yeah, yeah, it's OK, umm, we've had four successful brain transplants in the last week.

ICE CAT: *(Skeptical.)* Brain transplants?

HUNK: Oh, yeah. So when are we going to meet?

ICE CAT: Soon, I hope, you guys can't do brain transplants. They don't exist. All you can do is transplant tissue.

HUNK: *(Thinks.)* Uh, oh. *(Types.)* Well, that's what I meant, down at the hospital we call them brain transplants.

ICE CAT: How long have you been a doctor?

HUNK: *(Thinks.)* How old did I say I was? Oh, no I can't

remember…um… *(Types.)* Oh, um, since I was 26 so I guess four years.

ICE CAT: *(Thinks.)* What? I thought you were 34. *(Types.)* Are you really a doctor?

HUNK: Look. *(Pauses and sighs.)* I'm gonna be totally honest with you, I'm not. *(Pause. He thinks.)* Man, she's so cool, I hope… *(Types.)* Are you mad?

ICE CAT: No, no I'm not, I guess because I'm not really a model either. I'm sixteen.

HUNK: Hey, me too.

ICE CAT: Really?

HUNK: Really, and I'm actually from Winnipeg.

ICE CAT: *(Thinks.)* Wow, he's my age and from my town, maybe this can still work…*(Types.)* Yeah, me too, we should meet.

HUNK: *(Thinks.)* Wow, this is one awesome girl. I wonder where she is right now? *(Types.)* We should. Where are you now?

ICE CAT: Charleswood Library.

HUNK: *(Aloud.)* Charleswood?

ICE CAT: *(Hears this and they both look at each other.)*

They just stare shocked at each other.

The End.

Kaddy

HANNAH PRODAN

"This play won second place in 2004. It deals with suicide again, but from a different perspective. While it was ultimately edged out of first place by a more comedic piece, there is no denying that Kaddy had a powerful affect on the audience." —A.K.

> *The U.L. corner of the stage is lit up to show OLDER KAYLA sitting amidst a pile of boxes, rummaging through one in her lap. After a couple seconds she puts the box down and glances around.*

OLDER KAYLA: Dylan? Have you seen that letter from my editor around anywhere? I can't find it in here.

> *DYLAN enters, carrying another box. He sets it down beside OLDER KAYLA.*

DYLAN: This one's mostly important papers and letters, it might be in here.

OLDER KAYLA: Thanks, hun.

> *DYLAN leans down as OLDER KAYLA stretches up to give him a quick kiss on the cheek.*

DYLAN: I'm going to finish unpacking the dishes. Don't take too long looking or we'll miss the show.

> *DYLAN exits as OLDER KAYLA dumps the contents of the new box out in her lap. Among other papers is a small, folded piece of paper. She unfolds it and begins to read.*

> *The U.R. corner of the stage is illuminated to show KADDY sitting.*

KADDY: Dylan. I love you as much as anybody can love someone else, but I just can't do this anymore.

OLDER KAYLA: Shit…

                 OLDER KAYLA puts the paper aside and begins rummaging through the rest of the contents of the box. She pauses as her eyes dart back to the note. She sighs as she pulls the note towards her and resumes reading.

KADDY: I can't go through everyday pretending I'm happy. The truth is I'm not. I can't be. And I give up…

                 OLDER KAYLA keeps reading for a few minutes, then refolds the paper.

OLDER KAYLA: That's it? Ten years of wondering for that? You've got to be kidding me.

                 OLDER KAYLA pushes the box and its contents aside.

                 I thought I'd forgotten it all…

                 The lights on OLDER KAYLA fade out as lights illuminate center stage to show a sunny beach, mid-afternoon. KADDY and KAYLA are laying out on the dock in the middle, staring up at the sky.

                 OLDER KAYLA enters, D.L. and wanders over to the dock, watching the two younger girls.

KADDY: Check out that cloud, right there. What would you say it looks like?

KAYLA: Which one? Ooh! It's that dog from The Neverending Story. What was his name again? Falcon?

KADDY: Falkor. Yeah, I guess I can see that. I was thinking more along the lines of an Ewok, but Falkor works, too.

                 OLDER KAYLA glances up, caught up in the happiness of her old friend for a moment.

OLDER KAYLA: She's right. It really does look like an Ewok.

KADDY: You know what I really can't stand?

KAYLA: What? I mean, besides nothing.

KADDY: I'm serious, Kayla. I hate when people talk about guys and girls being soul mates.

KAYLA: What's wrong with that?

KADDY: I'm just saying that I don't think romance has anything to do with soul mates. I think it's really more about the connection than anything else. Kind of like what you and me have.

KAYLA hesitates, unsure of how to respond.

OLDER KAYLA: *(Walking down the dock towards the girls.)* Come on! Don't even think about ignoring it this time! Ask her what's up- you know something's up!

KADDY: Meh, just forget I said anything. I'm just rambling again. *(She glances back up at the sky.)* Hey! That one looks like a young John Cusack, wouldn't you say?

KAYLA: Nah, I'd say it's more of a George Clooney. Maybe even a Sean Connery, a lá James Bond, but not John Cusack.

KADDY: Whatever. Everyone's entitled to their own opinion, Kayla.

OLDER KAYLA: See! Right there! Normal people do not get upset over bullshit like that! They just don't! Open your damn eyes, would ya?

KAYLA: Um...I'm sorry?

KADDY glances down at her watch and jumps up.

KADDY: I've got to go. Sorry for snapping. It's just all this pressure with university admissions...

KAYLA: No, don't worry, I totally understand. Ahh... after this summer we've only got one more year and we can leave this place forever.

KADDY: Yeah, after this summer… *(She checks her watch again.)* Anyways! I'm really going to be late if I don't get going soon, so I'll see ya.

KAYLA: Later.

KADDY and KAYLA race to the end of the dock. After a brief goodbye, KADDY exits D.L. and KAYLA exits D.R. OLDER KAYLA watches KADDY for a second before turning her attention to KAYLA.

OLDER KAYLA: OK. First—Kaddy worried about university? Not highly likely with her grades. And second—see you? Where's the later? She always said later. Even if you're going to play dumb to everything else, you could've at least caught on to the absence of later.

The lights dim on center stage. The U.R. corner of the stage is illuminated to reveal KADDY sitting on the floor beside a bed. Next to her is a bottle of prescription pills. She has a notebook open in front of her and is writing hurriedly, pausing every so often to think.

OLDER KAYLA enters, D.R. For a moment she pauses, shocked, then rushes over to the bed.

No! No, no, no! This isn't going to happen again! This just can't happen. Just, stop! Kaddy! Stop thinking about yourself. How could you do this to me? Honestly, did you even stop to think about what this was going to do to me? Or Dylan? What about your parents?

KADDY stops writing for a second. She looks right at OLDER KAYLA for a moment, then goes back to writing.

Just stop to think about it before you do anything. Or, I don't know, maybe just stop thinking about it. *(She pauses as she looks at KADDY's eyes, then slides to the floor by the bed, turning to look at the audience.)* I know that look. Every time she set her mind on doing something, that same glimmer would show up in her eyes. Nothing could stop her from doing something once she'd decided that she had to do it.

> *KADDY carefully tears out three sheets of paper from the notebook, watching OLDER KAYLA the entire time. She folds the papers one by one, slowly and deliberately, as the lights fade.*

> *The lights brighten again to illuminate KAYLA sleeping restlessly on her bed. DYLAN approaches the bedroom tentatively, OLDER KAYLA follows a few feet behind him.*

DYLAN: Kayla? *(When there's no reply, he makes his way over to the bed and shakes KAYLA gently.)* Kayla, come on, wake up. It's about Kaddy.

OLDER KAYLA: How can you sleep? Your best friend—your soul mate for God's sake—just killed herself, and you're sleeping like a baby!

KAYLA: *(Rolling over.)* Dylan? Can I ask you a question?

DYLAN: OK…

KAYLA: What the hell are you doing in my bedroom? If you haven't noticed, it's like *(She pauses to glance over at her alarm clock.)* two in the morning. Ooh, wouldn't Kaddy be mad if she knew we were alone here this late?

DYLAN: Your parents let me in.

> *DYLAN turns and walks over to the dresser, unable to look at KAYLA.*

KAYLA: *(Sitting up.)* Dylan? What is it? What's wrong?

OLDER KAYLA: Soul mates! Damnit, you should know what's wrong!

DYLAN: *(Without turning around.)* She looked so happy. How sick is that? After what she did, how the fuck could she still look happy? It was just- yeah, it was sick.

KAYLA: Would you mind letting me join this conversation that you seem to be having with yourself?

DYLAN: Sure, why not. Kaddy's dead, Kayla. *(He turns around.)* She O.D.'d.

KAYLA: What do you mean she's dead?

OLDER KAYLA: He means she's dead because you wouldn't see all the signs she gave you guys!

DYLAN: I'm sorry, Kayla.

KAYLA: You didn't answer my question. How could you say she's dead?

DYLAN: I wish it wasn't true, but it is.

KAYLA: She isn't dead. Watch, I'll call her and prove it to you.

                    KAYLA reaches for the phone and begins to dial, but DYLAN takes it from her and hangs up.

                    I just saw her this afternoon. She said she'd see me later. Why would she say that if she knew there wouldn't be a later?

OLDER KAYLA: She said see ya. There was no later.

DYLAN: I wish I knew what to tell you, Kayla.

                    DYLAN puts an arm around KAYLA's shoulder and pulls her into a hug as the lights fade out.

                    The lights illuminate KAYLA's bedroom again. OLDER KAYLA is sitting on the bed. KAYLA is in the middle of the room, dancing to music playing on her mp3 player. DYLAN enters, pausing to watch KAYLA for a moment before reaching out and taking the headphones off of her ears.

KAYLA: What're you doing here?

DYLAN: That's your choice—we can talk about everything, or work on what we're going to say at the funeral. *(He tosses a notebook on the bed.)*

KAYLA: *(Throwing the notebook off the bed.)* I don't want to talk Dylan! And I don't want to work on anything for the funeral!

OLDER KAYLA: Of course you don't! You just want to waste the entire summer wallowing in self pity!

KAYLA: It hurts too much to think about her being gone. There's too many things about her that I'm going to miss. Like how happiness seemed so natural for her.

DYLAN: And I'm not going to miss those same things? Kayla, in case you've forgotten, I lost Kaddy, too.

KAYLA: It's not the same, Dylan. How can you be hurting so much if I haven't seen you cry once over this?

DYLAN: Because of you, Kayla. Because if I let how I feel show, then you'd be fucked. Nobody else was even near as close to her as you were, besides me and her parents. Nobody else is going to understand how you feel, Kayla. I do. It may not seem like it, but I do. Whether or not you can see it, you're falling apart. I already lost someone I cared about this summer, I'm not going to lose you, too.

KAYLA: What the hell is that supposed to mean, 'I'm not going to lose you, too'?

DYLAN: Look, I didn't mean I thought you were going to kill yourself. Believe it or not, Kayla, you can be dead while your heart's still beating.

KAYLA: What the hell are you talking about, Dylan?

OLDER KAYLA: If you'd just shut up for a minute, maybe he'd be able to tell you.

DYLAN: I'm talking about what happens if you keep on letting this control you like you have been. You're going to keep dragging yourself out of bed every day, and go through it all on autopilot. I don't want to see that happen to you.

KAYLA: What makes you such a goddamn expert?

OLDER KAYLA: He's trying to help. Why do you keep getting mad at him?

DYLAN: Just trust me. You don't want to fall into autopilot.

KAYLA: And why wouldn't I want to do that? 'Cause I sure as hell can't deal with this now. We're teenagers, Dylan. We're supposed to be dealing with—well, I don't know what we're supposed to be dealing with, but not this!

DYLAN: Maybe we shouldn't have to deal with it, but like it or not, we do. You can't just sweep all of this under some rug and hope you wake up tomorrow in the same safe world you knew when Kaddy was here.

                 KAYLA shoots DYLAN an angry look.

                 Come on, Kayla, you know it just as well as I do. While the rest of us have spent high school trying to find ourselves, you just hid behind Kaddy.

KAYLA: What are you trying to prove by accusing me of using Kaddy?

DYLAN: Fuck, Kayla, why the hell do you have to be so damn difficult? I'm trying to help you. But it's not going to work until you accept that life isn't some glass jar.

KAYLA: Don't get mad at me. You can't tell me you don't wish that things were a lot easier.

DYLAN: You know what? I do wish things weren't so hard. But they are. That's life. There's nothing we can do about it. So the way I see it, we have two choices. We either die like you're doing, or we accept things as they are and try to move on. Try to live.

KAYLA: Accept what, Dylan? I don't even know what I'm accepting yet! Kaddy killed herself.

DYLAN:	That's because you haven't tried to figure it out yet!
KAYLA:	That's all I've been doing for the past few days is trying to figure the whole damn situation out.
OLDER KAYLA:	Bullshit!
DYLAN:	But you haven't been!
OLDER KAYLA:	You spend all your time lying here on your bed with your music.
DYLAN:	You're lost in your own world, feeling sorry for yourself because now you're the unhappy one.
OLDER KAYLA:	You're not trying to figure things out, you're avoiding them.
DYLAN:	Tell me, Kayla—have you even once thought about how anybody else feels?
KAYLA:	Oh, that's just priceless, Dylan. You're calling me selfish. In case you've forgotten, Kaddy's the one that took those pills. And I'm the selfish one?
DYLAN:	I'm not saying that.
KAYLA:	What about you? Let me tell you why you didn't notice anything. You had the perfect high school romance with Kaddy, and if something was wrong with her, that would mess up what you had. You took advantage of her, too.
DYLAN and OLDER KAYLA:	Kayla!
OLDER KAYLA:	Why do you have to fight him so much? He's the only person that can help you, and you're treating him like shit for trying!
DYLAN:	Godamnit, Kayla! Get it through your fucking head. It's nobody's fault! Maybe I missed some signs—we all did. There's no point in thinking about what we could've done, because there's absolutely nothing we can do to bring her back.

KAYLA: Like making the best out of a bad situation?

DYLAN: Exactly like that.

KAYLA: Ha! Where's the best part about waking up every morning knowing your best friend killed herself? Knowing that she obviously didn't care about the rest of us as much as we cared about her?

> *DYLAN pulls KAYLA into a hug as she begins to cry and the lights fade out.*

> *Centre stage lights up to reveal the beach again.*

> *KAYLA and DYLAN enter, D.L., walking slowly along the beach. KAYLA is holding her shoes gingerly in one hand.*

Dylan...

> *KAYLA turns onto the dock, heading for the end. DYLAN follows, glancing her way, giving her a look to encourage her to continue.*

There wasn't anything we could've done, right?

> *KAYLA sits on the end of the dock, letting her feet hang over the edge. OLDER KAYLA enters, D.L., and pauses at the beginning of the dock.*

DYLAN: Nothing. You know that. She didn't want us to know. *(He crouches beside her.)* You were the best friend she could've ever hoped for. You were there for her every time. You always knew she was upset before I did, sometimes even before she did.

KAYLA: Except this time.

DYLAN: I didn't want to show you this before, because I wasn't sure you could handle it.

> *DYLAN pulls out his wallet, and from that, a folded piece of loose leaf.*

KAYLA: Dylan, no. I told you, I don't want to know why.

> DYLAN *picks up KAYLA's hands, putting the paper in it before closing her hand into a fist.*

DYLAN: It's not that note, Kayla. This one she wrote just for you.

> KAYLA *looks up at DYLAN, then down at her closed fist. DYLAN stands up, patting KAYLA gently on the shoulder before walking back to wait for her on the beach. The set dims, except for a spotlight on KAYLA as she opens her hand, unfolding the paper.*

> KADDY *enters, walking towards OLDER KAYLA as KAYLA begins to read the note.*

KADDY: Kayla—first, I want to say I'm sorry. You don't know how sorry I am for leaving you to deal with Peace Bay on your own. And I'm sorry for putting you through this.

OLDER KAYLA: Sorry? You've got to say a lot more than just sorry about this. 'Oh, sorry I killed myself' just doesn't cut it.

KADDY: I don't want you to feel guilty. It's not your fault—it's nobody's fault.

OLDER KAYLA: You're wrong. It's your fault. Nobody forced those pills down your throat. Only you did that.

KADDY: I want to thank you, Kayla. I couldn't have found a better best friend if I had tried. You were there for me too many times to count.

OLDER KAYLA: Most people say thanks with a card, and maybe some flowers. They don't usually kill themselves in gratitude.

KADDY: I want to say one more time that I really believe we are soul mates. You were there for me like I think only a soul mate could be.

OLDER KAYLA: If you knew we were soul mates, you would've known that you killed a part of me with you. Isn't that how the theory works? One soul isn't complete without the other?

KADDY: Take care of Dylan for me, will you? And make sure my parents get through this. I love you, Kay. Kaddy.

After a moment, KADDY turns and exits, leaving OLDER KAYLA standing alone.

KAYLA refolds the note and holds it for a minute. The spotlight fades away and the stage lights come back on, but only dim, to indicate a passing of time. From offstage comes a loon call. KAYLA and DYLAN both look outwards, towards the sound. KAYLA smiles as she gets up, and walks towards DYLAN. He nods and they join hands, exiting D.L. as the lights fade to black.

The lights brighten on an empty set. KAYLA is standing, waiting, as OLDER KAYLA enters and makes her way over.

OLDER KAYLA: You still think you've dealt with it, don't you?

KAYLA: Of course I have. I'm living my own life now, and I'm moving on.

OLDER KAYLA: You haven't dealt with it. It took me until graduation.

KAYLA: Me? What about you?

OLDER KAYLA: I have moved on. Dylan and I are together, we're happy. And I'm making a name for myself with my writing. Every day things get better.

KAYLA: Then why are you here? I know we're the ones you go to sleep thinking about. Dylan, and Kaddy, and me—or I guess you—ten years ago. You wake up from nightmares about us. We're always there, in your mind. We'll leave if you just ask; if you really want us to. It only takes a second. But you haven't asked.

OLDER KAYLA: You make it seem like you guys control me.

KAYLA: Don't we?

OLDER KAYLA: Not at all. I could've gotten rid of you guys years ago.
                You know why I didn't? Because I'm a writer. All you
                guys are to me now is inspiration for some fictional
                characters somewhere down the line.

KAYLA: I don't believe you. Just answer one question. Why
                haven't you gone back to Peace Bay for even a day
                since you graduated?

OLDER KAYLA: There's nothing there for me anymore. That's all.

KAYLA: Kaddy's there.

OLDER KAYLA: Kaddy's dead.

KAYLA: She's buried there, though. All your memories of her
                are there. Dylan's gone back.

OLDER KAYLA: There's nothing in Peace Bay for me to go back to.

KAYLA: But there's everything there for you to run away
                from.

                *KAYLA exits D.R., leaving OLDER KAYLA alone.
                The lights fade to black.*

                *The U.L. corner of the stage is lit up again to show
                OLDER KAYLA writing amidst the clutter of boxes.*

OLDER KAYLA: The night on the dock always seemed like a kind of
                last goodbye. It was so peaceful; I wondered if Kaddy
                was in a place just like it. I thought that was it for me.
                I honestly believed I had dealt with it all.

                DYLAN enters, putting on his coat.

DYLAN: Kayla? We're going to have to leave soon if we want
                to make the movie on time.

OLDER KAYLA: Alright. Give me five minutes and I'll be ready.

DYLAN: OK, I'll be outside waiting.

OLDER KAYLA: *(Writing.)* I really hadn't dealt with it, though. Now

I have. I've realized that even though I lost a friend then, I gained something more. My identity.

OLDER KAYLA closes the notebook and tosses it into one of the boxes. Grabbing her coat off one of the other boxes she exits.

The End.

Hockey Life in Canada

Devon Ford

"This play won second place in our fifth anniversary year. It lost a tight race for the inaugural Cora McKenzie Award For First Place to Dylan Gyles' first play. Both plays were excellent, and real crowd pleasers — and the voting could have gone either way. At the time, Devon said that he was a hockey player who had never thought of being a writer. He still plays hockey. I hope he still writes, too." —A.K.

Brad
Aaron
Derek

Act I

BRAD: Hockey's alright I guess. *(Speaking to his counselor.)*

AARON: I love hockey! *(Speaking to a reporter.)*

DEREK: I hate hockey. *(Speaking to a co-worker.)*

BRAD: I used to play…unfortunately I was introduced to Mr. Cocaine at a young age. I started liking it so much I started dealing and then…you know the story…got hooked on other drugs, got kind of careless, and now I'm here. Not everyone who does weed moves on to 'shrooms and then on to whatever, but that's just how it worked for me.

AARON: I have loved it since I can remember. Getting paid a million dollars a year to play a game! I'M THE LUCKIEST BASTARD IN THE WORLD!

DEREK: *(Reading a newspaper and having a smoke.)* What a sad excuse for a sport. What a bunch of wimps. They complain about every little thing. They complain about not getting paid enough. Rookies getting a million a year? Christ! I won't make that in my life.

BRAD: I was told I could have made it to the NHL but instead of working on my shot and fitness in the summers I'd work on getting fried. Yeah, I know, bad lifestyle choice. But when you are 17, on top of your game, with a trail of puck bunnies in your wake, you know, you feel…invincible.

AARON: Don't tell anyone, but…I would pay Vancouver to let me play for them. God it's sweet. I mean really! How can't you love it? It's the coolest game on earth! Did you see my face on the bicycle safety posters? Yeah, that's me. I even came up with the slogan. *(Proud smile.)* "I wear mine on and off the ice." Pretty good, eh?

DEREK: They'll never be satisfied. It's such a stupid game… pro-hockey. And greedy too. I had a friend who made it to the NHL. He's probably sucking about his million a year too. Boo hoo.

BRAD: What do I like about hockey? I used to love the tournaments where you'd have to stay in hotels. The mini-stick hockey games. They were the greatest. Even though it did get us kicked out of hotels. The workers would run after us 'cause when they told us to stop playing we would go somewhere else and play. We got lots of dirty looks from old people, and a few words exchanged with very sleepy truckers.

AARON: I wonder how my junior high teacher feels. I remember her telling me, "You're an embarrassment to your family and you're never going to do anything with your life and you're going to end up living as a bum on the street." Not in so many words… but something like that. She even told my mom to cancel her RESP's. I'd like to go back to Stelly's School and say, "LOOK AT ME NOW! I MADE THE NHL!" But that would be mean. I make more in one season that she makes in 25 years. You know, she always gave me homework when I was going on a road trip and if it wasn't done I'd get a detention. Some people don't understand how hard you have to work to make it. One in a million.

DEREK: Everyone was obsessed with playing mini stick. We played hockey all day then they get to the hotel and would want to play some more. I think the reason I hated it so much was probably my dad. He was my coach so there was no way of skipping out practices and games. Even when I told him I hated it, it was like he just decided not to hear me, as if my opinion didn't matter. If it was up to me I would have quit when I was ten.

BRAD: When I think back to it I really wish I would have just kept drinking. I could have done something with my life instead of wasting my time in this place. It's depressing, but I am not a write off yet. I'm in the best shape of my life. I think that as soon as I get out of this hellhole I'll try to start playing again…somewhere. I know my shot to the NHL is gone but…maybe I'll just play for some fun.

AARON: Minor hockey? Yeah…I wish I could have those times back. Where all skill levels played together and it didn't matter, it was just a game. The biggest thrill is striving to make it…once you are there it gets a little stale. If I don't produce every game I could be benched, sent down to the minors, or even traded. The pressure at contract time is huge. But all in all it's worth everything just to play and get paid…well.

DEREK: The only thing I ever liked about hockey was giving people big body checks and dropping the mitts. I didn't like those long road trips or hotels. You'd get on a bus at seven in the morning, travel five hours, then be too tired to play. A waste of a weekend. I could have been playing school sports like volleyball. Or basketball but I wasn't allowed to…because it would take too much time away from hockey. It was 300 bucks just to put me in, and another 600 for equipment.

BRAD: I'm holding up OK. I'll make the few weeks I have left, even with those creeps in the cell beside me. It makes for some very quick showers. The thought of it just makes me sick, then hearing it every night from people down the hall. Yeah, it's not too cool. These last days are going to be the hardest...you know... knowing how close I am to getting out. But I have something worth waiting to get out for. That's all I can think about. I imagine the sounds of the puck hitting the stick...the crackling of the ice...even the familiar smell of the change room! What I wouldn't give to get that all back. I never thought I'd regret anything. I used to think that no matter what happened I would be ok. But that's far from the truth.

AARON: Hockey players deserve every penny in their contracts. It's stressful. You can't spend too much time relaxing because you have to worry about staying in shape. It's hard for guys who have a family. You are on the road all the time with all kinds of...well...temptation. But without hockey I might have ended up being what my teacher said. Younger kids might think that being NHL would be the best life, but really it's not. Every game there's a risk that you could get a career ending injury. I don't think I have played long enough to be able to live off the money I have made yet. And I don't think I am prepared to go back to school if something goes wrong.

DEREK: Derek, Jr. wants to play hockey, but I think that academics are more important. That's why I've signed him up for Reach for the Top, and I'm going to help coach. He'll have much more fun in Reach for the Top anyway...I haven't heard of any Reach for the Top bunnies either.

BRAD: I've finished my Grade 12 with Honours right here. And I have started university. Guess what this is?

(Holds up a book.) Criminology. That's right, an ex-con studying to see what went wrong with his life. Pretty much everyone in here is a lifer. They don't have a life sentence, but you just know they are going to be in and out of jail for the rest of their lives. Not me...I'm never coming back.

DEREK: University was a blessing for me. I could finally quit hockey. I went to University of Alberta instead of UBC because UBC was too close to my dad. School is the most important thing when you're young. That's why I enrolled Derek Jr. in a private school. He thinks that he will miss his friends when he goes to his new school. But he'll make new ones. And it's not about having lots of friends that counts, it's the quality.

AARON: I don't have a safety net. No savings, no wife, no kids, no support network. If this lockout continues, I don't know what I'll do. Is there life after hockey? I guess I might find out. You know what's sad? The last book I read was Lord of the Flies, and that was in high school. Good thing I'm a good copier. I would have been screwed.

BRAD: I got a letter today, and there's a team reunion for my Peewee hockey team! I'm not sure what exactly we're doing, but hopefully I'll be able to play a bit of hockey. It's going to be weird seeing all those guys again. I haven't seen most of them since the end of that season. Aaron and Derek...my old linemates. I wonder what they're like.

AARON: I got an interesting letter today. It was from the coach of my Peewee team. He was telling me abut a team reunion from when we won the Provincials. Sounds like it could be fun. Could bring back some good memories from back in the minor hockey days. It will be kind of fun to find out how the guys have made out. It is difficult to connect with your pre-NHL life... but we all have to make the adjustment.

DEREK: My dad is organizing a little get together for my Peewee hockey team. You know, my dad turns 60 next year and he is still coaching minor hockey...I don't know what to think of this whole reunion. It would be kind of fun to see all the guys again. What do I have to talk about? How hockey ruined my life? I don't know, it might be OK. Maybe I won't be the only person who doesn't play anymore. I missed everything when we were younger, and I'm not missing this. My dad can't mess it up for me anymore.

Act II

At the party.

AARON: Hey, boys.

BRAD: Hey!

DEREK: Long time no see...so...what have you done these... well...past 15 years?

BRAD: Hard to believe...15 years plus...it seems like yesterday... I played some Bantam and Midget, and then made it to Jr. A. While I was playing Junior. I got cut because of some tomahawk incident. Don't remember it though.

AARON: Sounds like you. Derek?

DEREK: House league. *(AARON and BRAD laugh.)* At the highest level though. There were a lot of good players. They just didn't want to play Junior. Not everyone can just drop what he is doing...you know...if you have a kid.

AARON: You had a kid?! When?

DEREK: A boy. Grad 11. It sucked...when I was 17. But I must admit, being a dad is something I've grown into. I love him...but...I wouldn't recommend it as a lifestyle choice for teenagers.

BRAD: What's his name?

AARON: Let me guess! Derek...Derek junior! *(AARON and BRAD laugh.)* Well, I went on to play Bantam AAA, then took the big step to the WHL when I was 16. It was tons of fun in the 'Dub". The bus rides, girls and the parties. The pay sucked...but it didn't matter... everything was taken care of by my team. Easy living.

BRAD: Sweet.

             DEREK rolls his eyes.

AARON: What did you do after you got cut from Jr. A.

BRAD: Let's see. I spent a lot of time indoors. And a lot of time working out.

             Long pause.

AARON: Don't tell me...jail?

DEREK: Jail? What! What for?

BRAD: Fuelling my coke habit. Funding it really... *(Awkward silence.)*

AARON: Do you remember when you mooned the girls team but it was actually the nursery school bus?

DEREK: You mooned a nursery school?

BRAD: Yeah. Not on purpose though! That's the stuff of nightmares. Those poor kids.

AARON: You scarred me for life too. Do you remember the sky dump?

BRAD: Actually, I'm proud of that one. How many guys have the superhuman strength to straddle a bathroom stall and take a dump... Aaron...and hit the bowl every time. Not many...I'll give you that one.

DEREK: Boy, we were immature.

AARON: You boys look pretty thirsty. Let me buy you a beer.

BRAD:	Oh, thanks, man.
DEREK:	That's OK. I'll get my own.
AARON:	No, no, I got it.
DEREK:	It's OK. I can afford my own beer.
AARON:	Come on, I had a good year.
BRAD:	*(Jokingly.)* You call five goals a year a good year?
AARON:	$150,000 a goal after taxes is a pretty good year from where I'm standing. I'm not saying you can't afford a beer, it's just easier for me.
DEREK:	Same old hotshot…
AARON:	Whatever, man, buy your own beer. Maybe you should get your dad to buy it for you.
DEREK:	What do you mean?
AARON:	You know what I mean.
DEREK:	No, I don't know what you mean.
AARON:	Well…I mean…you must know…the only reason you were on this team was because of your old man.
DEREK:	Fuck you!
BRAD:	That's not true… OK boys, that's enough *(Gets between them.)* Keep your dicks in your pants.
DEREK:	There's only one dick here. *(Points to AARON. Silence.)*
BRAD:	If anyone has a right to complain it's me. You should try living in a box for a few months and just see if you could handle it.
DEREK:	You made that choice. You only have yourself to blame. You know. Do the crime, do the time.
AARON:	He's got a point.

BRAD: It could have been you, you were right there behind
             me every step in Junior…

AARON: Yes, sort of…but I knew when to draw the line and
             when to ride it.

BRAD: You are a dick.

AARON: Grow up, I made it, you didn't. Let's just have a couple
             beer and forget all this.

DEREK: Nah, I think I'm going home. I've got the morning
             shift.

BRAD: Oh there's a surprise.

DEREK: Surprise?

BRAD: A little adversity won't kill you. You don't need to
             bail.

DEREK: Better a quitter than a con.

AARON: Not cool.

BRAD: Anything else to say? Maybe you would like to take
             this outside?

             BRAD flexes like he is ready to fight.

DEREK: Sorry, I was out of line. See you guys around…

AARON: Here we go again…

DEREK: What?

AARON: What were you saying sorry for?

DEREK: For being a prick?

AARON: You were only stating a fact.

BRAD: I wasn't always the ex-con. Don't forget who the
             leading scorer was.

AARON: That was then…

There is a long pause. They are not able to look at each other. BRAD reaches into his bag and pulls out 3 mini-hockey sticks and a ball. He hands one to AARON and one to DEREK. For a moment they stare at the sticks, each smiles. BRAD drops the ball, they immediately begin to play...shouting and laughing and playing hard.

The End.

Think, Then Speak

Dylan Gyles

"This was the second of three plays written by Dylan Gyles to win the Cora McKenzie Award for First Place. Stylistically, it lies somewhere between the first one (his most straight forward) and the third one (his most challenging). Given the space, we could have happily published all three. A winning streak like Dylan's has never been (and may never be) repeated." —A.K.

Scene One

> *The stage is divided into two areas. Upstage is the high school hallway. DWIGHT and MIKE are on one side and SARAH is on the other. Downstage is inside DWIGHT's mind. DOCTOR is sitting and watching DWIGHT, he has an empty chair next to them.*

DWIGHT: There she is, the girl of my dreams, she—

MIKE: *(Smacks DWIGHT lightly.)* Dwight, you're thinking out loud again.

DWIGHT: Oh. Shit.

> *The scene freezes. DWIGHT walks down stage and is now speaking in his head.*

There she is, the girl of my dreams. Right now anyways. I've actually had a number of girls of my dreams, but they never last long. She's different though. Kind of...well, crazy, but I think I like that. I'm going to make a move soon...I just don't know what it'll be. *(Moves back upstage, the scene unfreezes.)*

MIKE: Honestly, who thinks out loud? How is that even a thing?

DWIGHT:	It's my therapist's idea. He says it'll help me, you know, get stuff out.
MIKE:	Well it is. You've got to learn to shut that off when you're with people though, because you sound like an insane person.
DWIGHT:	Mike's a good friend, he just—
MIKE:	Dude! Seriously!
DWIGHT:	Fuck. *(Moves down stage.)* Mike's my…only friend actually. See, everyone here has heard the story about what I did at my old school. In some versions I bit off a kid's nose like in *Batman Returns*. Rumours like that don't make you popular. Me and Mike were friends before all that though, he's probably the only one in the school who knows what actually happened. *(Moves back upstage.)*
MIKE:	You are a very insane person.
DWIGHT:	So you keep saying.

       SARAH closes her locker and walks past them.

	Hey, Sarah. *(SARAH smiles and keeps walking, he stares after her until she's gone.) (Moves downstage.)* See, what does that mean? I've known her for long enough to deserve more than just smile. What is that? *(Moves back upstage.)*
MIKE:	Weak. Shall I translate that little move of hers for you? "I don't want to go out with you, because you're very homosexual."
DWIGHT:	This coming from the guy who cried during *Free Willy*.
MIKE:	You can't use that every time!
DWIGHT:	I can and will.
MIKE:	I was having a really bad day, and my pet goldfish had just died that morning, and—whatever, forget it.

DWIGHT: I can't, it's stained in my memory.

MIKE: Try. And try to forget about Sarah too. You should find a girl who isn't…crazy.

DWIGHT: Why would I want that? I'm crazy, and opposites don't attract.

MIKE: They say they do.

DWIGHT: They are wrong, just like they always are. They were the ones who said that it's impossible to count the number of licks to the centre of a tootsie-pop, and I proved them wrong didn't I?

MIKE: One hundred and twelve—

DWIGHT: One hundred and twelve! They were also the ones who said that bullies will back down as soon as you stand up to them, and that people will like you for who you really are, and that an apple a day keeps the doctor away, and I proved every one of those wrong, didn't I?

MIKE: You sure did. Come on, class is starting.

DWIGHT: Oh, uh, I'm just going to go to the cafeteria or something.

MIKE: Why?

DWIGHT: I have English.

MIKE: Oh. Corey's still—

DWIGHT: Yep.

MIKE: Man, why don't you just tell the teacher or—

DWIGHT: Mike, please don't. I've thought about everything, I've tried everything. There's nothing I can do about it, okay? So just leave it alone.

MIKE: But Dwight, you could just—

DWIGHT: Mike.

MIKE: Alright. See ya. *(Exits.)*

DWIGHT: *(Begins to leave then stops. He sighs.)* I wouldn't get any work done anyways, he's just going to pull all the same shit, so don't go. *(Exits. He re-enters and crosses to the other side of the stage.)* Stupid, stupid, stupid, this is stupid. *(Exits.)*

Scene Two

Upstage is a memory of DWIGHT's house. GREG is lying on the couch, asleep. Downstage is in DWIGHT's mind. DOCTOR is sitting in his chair.

DWIGHT enters downstage sits in the chair next to DOCTOR.

DOCTOR: How are things, Dwight?

DWIGHT: Fine. Actually I don't think there's really a point in doing this today.

DOCTOR: This is all your idea. This helps, you know it does. Start with school.

DWIGHT: School was—

DOCTOR: Don't say fine. Think. Then talk it out.

DWIGHT: Sarah didn't talk to me. I said hi to her and she just walked right past me.

DOCTOR: Maybe she didn't hear you.

DWIGHT: No she heard me, she 'smiled, but she didn't say anything.

DOCTOR: Is that so bad?

DWIGHT: No I guess it's not. Can we stop now?

DOCTOR: No. The point of this is to look back and see things from a different perspective, not briefly sum it up. You're usually eager to do this, so what's different today?

DWIGHT: It was just a bad day today.

DOCTOR: Very bad?

DWIGHT: Yes.

DOCTOR: Terrible? *(DWIGHT sighs loudly.)* OK. So keep going through the day. What happened in English?

DWIGHT: Corey stole my test.

DOCTOR: He copied you again?

DWIGHT: No, he literally stole it. He waited until I was finished and then took it off my desk.

DOCTOR: But…what did you say when your teacher asked for your test?

DWIGHT: I told him I ate it.

DOCTOR: Why would you tell him that?

DWIGHT: Because I wouldn't put it past Mr. Clark to do a cavity search if I told him I shoved it up my ass.

DOCTOR: Dwight, you realize Corey is trying to see how far he can push you when he does something like that.

DWIGHT: Yes, I know.

DOCTOR: Well then why didn't you just tell Mr. Clark that he stole your test?

DWIGHT: Why do you think? You know the way it works. If I do anything or tell anyone then he'll wait till after school and beat me half to death.

DOCTOR: He wouldn't do that.

DWIGHT: Yes he definitely would.

DOCTOR: Then he would be expelled at the least.

DWIGHT: Yes, and if that happened, he would find me and beat me half to death again. And I think getting beaten half to death twice, means I'm fully dead.

DOCTOR: Do you actually believe he would kill you?

DWIGHT: Yes, I know he would, okay?! He would go to jail laughing, if it was because I was dead! There is no way out. I'm stuck, until he graduates or I do.

DOCTOR: If you keep letting him steal your tests, it'll be him before you.

DWIGHT: I'm aware of that, I've accepted that. Can we please move on?

DOCTOR: Alright. So, what happened when you got home?

                DWIGHT walks upstage and acts out the memory.

DWIGHT: I just went to bed. *(Begins to cross the stage.)*

DOCTOR: What about your brother?

DWIGHT: *(Stops mid-step. He turns around and sees GREG on the couch. He moves to try and hide him from DOCTOR.)* He wasn't there today.

DOCTOR: It's Thursday, he's always there.

DWIGHT: *(Steps aside so DOCTOR can see him.)* He was asleep.

DOCTOR: You said he always wakes up.

DWIGHT: Do we really have to do this?

DOCTOR: Yes. If you don't get it out now, you'll just push it down and make it worse.

DWIGHT: Fine. *(Walks back to the edge of the couch and sees GREG. He tries to tip toe past and is just about to exit.)*

GREG: *(Still lying down with his eyes closed.)* Where are you going Dwight-fuck?

DWIGHT: *(Stops and turns around.)* To my room. I'm tired.

GREG: *(Sits up.)* No actually you're not, Dwight-fuck.

DWIGHT: Is that really the best you can come up with? Dwight-fuck?

GREG: *(Stands up.)* Oh I'm sorry Dwight-fuck, I won't call you Dwight-fuck anymore. So where's the money Dwight-Fuck?

DWIGHT: Not today Greg.

GREG: Yep, today Dwight-fuck.

DWIGHT: You have a job! Where's your money?

GREG: I have to pay the bills for this piece of shit house that you live in. So if you want to start paying them, be my guest. Until then, your money is mine.

DWIGHT: No it's not. *(GREG takes a step towards him, and DWIGHT puts up a fist.)* Don't!

GREG: Are you kidding me. OK, hit me Dwight-fuck.

> *Moves toward DWIGHT. DWIGHT punches but GREG catches it and twists it around his back.*

Now give me the money or I'll break it.

> *DWIGHT pulls a few bills out of his pocket and throws them on the floor. GREG releases him.*

Pick them up. *(DWIGHT doesn't move. GREG takes a step towards him. DWIGHT picks up the bills and puts them in GREG's hand.)*

DWIGHT: I hate you. I wish mom was still here.

GREG: No, you don't. You didn't have to deal with her. You didn't know what she was really like. She was a drunken, abusive, bitch.

DWIGHT: Well, start drinking a little more and you've got her down pat.

GREG: If she had stayed, it would have only been to kill you. She hated you more then I do, and that was before what you did. *(DWIGHT looks hurt. He moves to the couch and sits down.)* ...Look, I didn't mean what you did, I just... *(Exits.)*

DOCTOR: Does he often bring up Susie?

DWIGHT: *(Moves back down stage and sits in his chair.)* No. He knows he shouldn't talk about her.

DOCTOR: He seemed sorry afterwards.

DWIGHT: He didn't know her. He was never around when she was here. And if you don't know her, you don't have the right to talk about her.

DOCTOR: Yes, that's true. Why do you think he brought her up?

DWIGHT: I don't usually bring up mom.

DOCTOR: So why did you today?

DWIGHT: I don't know. I just did.

DOCTOR: Yes, in the heat of the moment you 'just do' something, that's why you're sitting here now. So you can think about why you did it.

DWIGHT: I was just fed up with it today. With all of it.

DOCTOR: You know you can always—

DWIGHT: —Don't. I don't want to be taken away, I don't want foster parents, I don't want anything to happen to Greg. I just want to put up with him until high school's over and then move out. That's it.

DOCTOR: Alright. Do you think you're ready to talk about Susie yet?

DWIGHT: No.

DOCTOR: That's fine. Whenever you're ready is fine.

           Beat.

DWIGHT: By the way, I think I've permanently disabled my inner monologue thanks to you.

DOCTOR: Well that's good.

DWIGHT: How is that good? It's going to get me beaten up.

DOCTOR: Well, if there was someone who you had problems communicating your feelings for, you might accidentally let something slip in front of them. That might ease things along with her.

DWIGHT: Or it might just terrify her.

DOCTOR: Yes, that's the other possibility.

Scene Three

> Upstage is the high school hallway. DWIGHT and SARAH are standing by their lockers. Downstage is in DWIGHT's mind. DOCTOR is sitting in his chair.
>
> DWIGHT and SARAH make eye contact. DWIGHT tries to say something, but gives up.

SARAH: So I almost got run over today.

DWIGHT: What?

SARAH: Yeah, I was riding my bike down across a back alley and this black car came speeding out and threw me like ten feet forward.

DWIGHT: (Pauses, waiting for more of the story.) That's it?

SARAH: Yeah that's it. What more do you want?

DWIGHT: Well you can't just finish a story like that! I mean…are you OK?

SARAH: I don't know. Do I look dead at all? I can't really tell.

DWIGHT: I guess not. Turn around.

SARAH: (Turns around.) Do I look deader from behind?

DWIGHT: Oh, no. I just wanted to see your ass.

SARAH: (Turns back to face him.) You dirty, dirty boy.

The scene freezes, except for DWIGHT.

DOCTOR: Wait. You actually said to her…"I wanted to see your ass"?

DWIGHT: Well, I just figured it was time to make my intentions known.

DOCTOR: Yes but…"I wanted to see your ass"?

DWIGHT: Well it worked, so shut up.

The scene unfreezes.

So, did the driver do anything?

SARAH: Yeah, he got out of his car, and started screaming at me for getting in the way.

DWIGHT: He got mad at you for getting hit by his car?

SARAH: Yep, he told me I should watch where I was going.

DWIGHT: What did you say?

SARAH: I told him I was offended, because I was visually impaired. And then I told him I was suing and gave him a fake number where he could get in touch with my lawyer.

DWIGHT: And he believed you?

SARAH: I think so, because he looked really scared.

The scene freezes.

DOCTOR: This girl is insane.

DWIGHT: Shush!

DOCTOR: Sorry.

The scene unfreezes.

DWIGHT: You're insane.

SARAH: Thanks, I try.

DWIGHT: You succeed... She's really beautiful.

SARAH: Um. What?

            The scene freezes.

DOCTOR: Oh! Hold the phone! I thought you said that it was a bad idea. That it would just terrify her.

DWIGHT: It was an accident.

DOCTOR: I'm sure.

            The scene unfreezes.

SARAH: What was that? Were you narrating your life?

DWIGHT: Uh... No. I just uh... *(Laughs awkwardly.)* See my therapist thought it would be a good idea to think out loud some times and it just kind of—

SARAH: Wow, talking about your therapist, that's a real turn on.

DWIGHT: Yeah. Uh...

            The scene freezes. DWIGHT glares at DOCTOR. DOCTOR shrugs and looks embarrassed.

DOCTOR: Sorry.

            The scene unfreezes.

SARAH: So you're like, terrible at hitting on girls huh?

DWIGHT: Well...yeah. Sorry.

SARAH: Like, I've heard a lot of bad pickup lines, but "my therapist said"?

DWIGHT: Yeah. *(Looks around uncomfortably and tries to slowly turn away from her.)*

SARAH: *(Laughs and pulls him back to face her.)* Relax, Dwight, I'm just screwing with you. *(Kisses him on the cheek and starts to leave.)* You can take me out this weekend. *(Exits.)*

DOCTOR: The classic "My therapist said" line. Works every time.

DWIGHT: *(Moves downstage.)* I'm sorry I doubted you.

DOCTOR: Oh no, please. I insist you take full credit for whatever that was.

DWIGHT: Yeah, I guess I was pretty amazing there.

MIKE: Hey Dwight. So what was going on there with Sarah?

DWIGHT: *(Moves back upstage.)* Well, I'll have you know, I just kinda asked her out sort of.

MIKE: What?! How? What did she say?

DWIGHT: Oh, I won't bore you with details. You know, just gave her the eye.

MIKE: Yeah, I'm sure. I'll bet you said something creepy and weird.

DWIGHT: Pfft... Nah.

              The DOCTOR nods his head.

MIKE: I have to get to class, I want the real story later. (He exits)

DOCTOR: So things are looking up, huh?

DWIGHT: Yeah, I guess they are. So should I call her, or—

COREY: *(Enters.)* Who are you talking to Dwight?

DWIGHT: No one. *(Turns around and tries to get away, but COREY grabs him by shoulder and pulls him back.)*

COREY: Whoa, whoa, slow down. I just want to talk to you. You know what we have to talk about right? You weren't in class yesterday.

              DWIGHT looks over at DOCTOR helplessly. DOCTOR looks away, then rises and quickly exits.

DWIGHT: Corey, do we have to do this now?

COREY:.   You know what happened in English? We had a quiz on *Great Expectations*. Guess how that went.

DWIGHT: I'm sorry. I was sick okay.

COREY: *(Squeezes DWIGHT's shoulder and forces him to his knees.)* I failed the quiz, Dwight. Now do I have to remind you what happens if I fail this course?

DWIGHT: No.

COREY: Good. So if you understand that, why did you purposefully skip today?

DWIGHT: Look Corey, I'm sorry, but I really was sick this morning— *(COREY squeezes harder, and he cries out in pain.)*

COREY: That's bullshit, Dwight. I'm not a retard and when you treat me like a retard, I get pissed off. Now believe me when I say I can make your life a lot worse. So use your head, OK? *(Releases his grip and exits.)*

Scene Four

Upstage is DWIGHT's house. DWIGHT and MIKE are sitting on the couch. Downstage left is inside DWIGHT's mind. DOCTOR is sitting in the chair. Downstage right is DWIGHT's memory of Subway. SARAH is sitting at a table.

MIKE: Quit stalling, just tell me what happened!

DWIGHT: Don't rush me! *(He gets up and sits down at the table.)* OK, so we went to Subway for dinner—

MIKE: Ooh, you know how to impress the ladies!

DWIGHT: Shut up. She even said:

SARAH: I really like Subway.

DWIGHT: Yeah me too…

>   *Beat.*

MIKE: …And?

DWIGHT: Well I was really nervous!

MIKE: So you just didn't say anything?

DWIGHT: I can't think of anything to say! *(Turns to DOCTOR.)* What should I say?

>   *Beat.*

DOCTOR: *(Realizes DWIGHT is talking to him.)* Me? I don't know, don't ask me.

DWIGHT: Well I've got literally nothing here! Just give me anything!

SARAH: You know most dates I've been on have involved some sort of talking.

DWIGHT: Yeah, sorry. I'm just kind of nervous I guess.

SARAH: Well don't be. You talk to me lots of times, this is no different.

DWIGHT: I beg to differ.

SARAH: Well I'm not going to say another word until you say something.

DWIGHT: OK…

>   *Long beat.*

MIKE: How long could you possibly go without saying anything?!

DWIGHT: Seven minutes.

MIKE: Seven?!

DWIGHT: Yeah, I kept checking the clock.

DOCTOR: It's been eight minutes!

DWIGHT: It's only been seven, and I'm waiting on you! What can I say to her?!

MIKE: Anything! You could have said anything!

DWIGHT: I can't say just anything, it's got to be something… good.

DOCTOR: No it doesn't! At this point, it just has to be words!

DWIGHT: But I want our first date to be…you know. Come on, you've got to give me something!

DOCTOR: Dwight… We don't do it this way. I can't.

DWIGHT: Yes you can, you're smarter than me, please!

DOCTOR: Alright. Say… Say…

MIKE: Well?

SARAH: Well?

DWIGHT: Well?

DOCTOR: Say you're obsessed with her.

DWIGHT: I'm obsessed with you.

SARAH: What?

MIKE: What?!

DWIGHT: *(Looks at DOCTOR who is speechless and shrugs. He looks back at SARAH.)* Uh…sorry, I just… Wow. That was a really weird thing to say, huh?

SARAH: Yeah, it was. I mean, it's kind of sweet, I guess, in a Norman Bates kind of way…

DWIGHT: Good that's what I was going for. He's kind of my role model.

SARAH: Aw, that's nice. It's good to have someone to look up to. How's the impression of your mother coming along?

DWIGHT: Well I live with my brother, so I'm kind of screwed for that aspect.

MIKE: No, wait. Wait, wait. So...the conversation just continued on like that?

DWIGHT: Yeah, pretty much. We kept talking, and then I walked her home after.

> DWIGHT and SARAH get up and walk to the side of the stage. SARAH kisses DWIGHT on the cheek then exits. DWIGHT moves back upstage.

MIKE: You... Are... A god!

DWIGHT: Yeah, I guess I am.

MIKE: Seriously, I can't believe she didn't run out of there screaming. Why did you say that?

DWIGHT: *(Looks at DOCTOR.)* I don't know.

> The scene freezes. DWIGHT moves down stage and sits in the chair next to DOCTOR.

Why did I say that?

DOCTOR: Look, I'm sorry. People say stupid things some times.

DWIGHT: Yes, but...from you? I don't know if I would have come up with that on my own.

DOCTOR: You did come up with it on your own though. Anything I think of, you thought of. You know that.

DWIGHT: Yeah, I guess.

DOCTOR: What's on your mind here Dwight?

DWIGHT: What if I'm crazy? Like actually crazy.

DOCTOR: You're not crazy.

DWIGHT: How do you know? If I'm crazy, so are you. So how can I trust anything you say?

DOCTOR: Dwight, we're not crazy. Crazy people don't think like we do. You put me here, to help clear things up. Think things through after they've happened. When you mess with our system and put me on the spot like that, we're bound to come up with some less than intelligent ideas.

DWIGHT: Yeah…yeah, of course.

DOCTOR: I think we should talk about Susie now.

DWIGHT: I really don't see what good that can do. I've made peace with it. Why mess with that?

DOCTOR: Never thinking about it is not making peace with it. You have to deal with it to get over it.

            Beat.

DOCTOR: I'll start. Whose fault was it?

DWIGHT: I know…

DOCTOR: Then say it out loud.

Scene Five

            Upstage is DWIGHT's house. MIKE and SARAH are sitting on the couch in awkward silence. Downstage right is DWIGHT's room. DWIGHT is sitting in a chair with his head in his hands. Downstage left is inside DWIGHT's mind, DOCTOR is sitting in the chair.

MIKE: Just give him another minute, he'll be fine.

SARAH: Yeah…

GREG: *(Enters stage left. He sees MIKE and SARAH and looks confused.)* Where's Dwight?

MIKE: Oh, hi Greg. He's in his room.

               GREG exits and re-enters downstage in DWIGHT's room. He and DWIGHT argue silently.

SARAH: OK Mike, you have to tell me what's going on with Dwight.

MIKE: I really think Dwight should be the one to.

SARAH: But he won't! He never tells me anything. Whenever I ask, he just goes off to be alone somewhere, like this. Please?

               GREG hits DWIGHT in the face. DWIGHT falls to the ground. He pulls a few bills out of his pocket and throws them at GREG. GREG takes the bills and exits.

MIKE: Well…I mean, you've probably heard the rumours, right?

SARAH: I heard that he killed a kid at his old school, but I know that's not true.

               GREG enters upstage and exits again.

MIKE: No, it's not, but he did beat the kid up really badly. He put him in the hospital.

SARAH: Really? Why?

MIKE: He over heard him making some terrible joke about Susie.

SARAH: Oh…

MIKE: *(Sees that she doesn't understand.)* Do you… Has he not told you about his sister?

SARAH: Well no, but—

MIKE: Oh shit, we really shouldn't be talking about this.

SARAH: But Mike, I just want to help—

MIKE: I'm sorry I promised… *(DWIGHT exits and re-enters upstage clutching his eye. MIKE and SARAH don't see him.)* He really didn't tell you anything about her?

DWIGHT: No, I didn't.

SARAH: Oh my God, are you OK?

DWIGHT: I can't believe you were going to tell her.

MIKE: What? No, I wasn't. She was just asking and I thought she already knew.

DWIGHT: I think you should get out now.

MIKE: Come on man, I really wasn't—

DWIGHT: Get out!

MIKE: But... OK, fine. *(Exits.)*

SARAH: What happened to you?

DWIGHT: You should leave too.

SARAH: No, I'm not going to.

DWIGHT: Yes you are. I want to be alone right now.

SARAH: You can't keep doing this Dwight! Being alone doesn't help. Talk to me!

DWIGHT: I don't want to talk to you!

SARAH: You have to talk to someone——

DWIGHT: Leave me alone.

          SARAH slowly gets her jacket on and exits.

DOCTOR: *(Stands up and walks to DWIGHT.)* Why are you taking this from Greg? He's stealing your money, he's beating you up, and now he's splitting up you and Sarah!

DWIGHT: There's nothing I can do about it!

DOCTOR: You could stand up for yourself! You could fight back!

DWIGHT: No, I can't. *(He points to his eye.)*

DOCTOR: Well then make it a fair fight.

DWIGHT: How?

DOCTOR: Anything…a knife!

DWIGHT: A knife?! You want me to stab my brother?

DOCTOR: No, of course not, that would be insane. I'm talking about scaring him.

DWIGHT: Scaring him? *(Considering.)* …No, I can't believe I'm even thinking about this.

DOCTOR: But you are thinking about it. You have to work hard all the time, but you're poor and failing school because of assholes like Corey and Greg. What if you could scare them just enough to make them to leave you alone?

DWIGHT: It's too dangerous.

DOCTOR: How is it dangerous? You're smart and responsible. You would obviously never actually use it.

DWIGHT: Obviously.

DOCTOR: Obviously! You would just let them know you have it and that would be enough.

DWIGHT: It's not like I would ever think of really using it.

DOCTOR: Of course not. So why not?

DWIGHT: Because. What if I'm crazy?

DOCTOR: If you can ask that question, do you really think you are?

Scene Six

> *Upstage is the high school hallway. Downstage is inside DWIGHT's mind. DOCTOR is sitting in the chair.*
>
> *DWIGHT enters. He looks around.*

DOCTOR: Stop looking for her. You don't have to apologize.

DWIGHT: Yes I do, I was acting like an asshole.

DOCTOR: She shouldn't have been asking about Susie. She had no right.

DWIGHT: She didn't even know about Susie.

DOCTOR: If she hasn't learned by now that she shouldn't have been prying into your life, then you don't need her.

DWIGHT: No. I have to fix things between us now, or I might lose her…if I haven't already.

COREY: *(Enters and shoves DWIGHT from behind him.)* Where the hell have you been?

DWIGHT: Oh shit.

COREY: Oh shit is right. Where the fuck have you been this week?! Finals are next week, do you know what that means?

DOCTOR: Are you just going to take this? Tell him to fuck off!

DWIGHT: OK Corey, fine. I can't do this right now though, I'm busy. *(Tries to walk past COREY.)*

COREY: What?! *(He grabs DWIGHT by the arm and pulls him back.)* What do you mean you're busy? Who do you think you're talking to?

DWIGHT: Corey, not now! *(Rips free of his grip.)*

COREY: Whoa! Since when did you become the physical type?

DOCTOR: He's mocking you! Do something!

COREY: Oh, are you going to go all psycho on me now? Like with that other guy?

DOCTOR: Why are you just standing there? Clenching your fists and biting your tongue doesn't mean anything to this guy. Do something! *(He stands up and begins circling DWIGHT.)*

COREY: *(DWIGHT tries to walk away, COREY steps in his way.)* They say you messed that kid up pretty bad. Now why was that again? Oh, I remember-

DWIGHT: —Stop! Corey, stop!

DOCTOR: Dwight, he's not going to stop, you have to make him!

COREY: It was because he made a joke about how you killed your sister.

DOCTOR: Did you hear that? Did you hear that?! He's talking about Susie. For God's sake Dwight we have to do something!

DWIGHT: I swear to God, Corey, I'm gonna—

COREY: What? What are you going to do Dwight?

DOCTOR: Show him! Open your bag and show him!

          DWIGHT begins to leave, COREY and DOCTOR follow.

COREY: Where the fuck do you think you're going, get back here!

          They all exit.

          (Off stage.) Hey, I'm talking to you... Oh, what the hell is that?

          A gunshot is heard. DOCTOR quietly walks back on stage and sits in the chair. After a few seconds DWIGHT enters holding a gun.

DWIGHT: What did you do?

DOCTOR: Me? Nothing. I was sitting here the entire time.

DWIGHT: No. No, you made me.

DOCTOR: How can I make you do something? You made yourself do it.

MIKE: *(Enters.)* Hey Dwight, what's going on?... Holy shit. What is this?

> *DWIGHT runs off stage.*

> *(Sees COREY off stage and runs to him.)* Oh jesus... Corey? *(Exits.)*

Scene Seven

> *Upstage is DWIGHT's house. DWIGHT is pacing back and forth. Downstage is inside DWIGHT's mind. DOCTOR sits in the chair.*

DWIGHT: Shit, shit, shit.

DOCTOR: Calm down. You haven't done anything wrong.

DWIGHT: I brought a gun to school!

DOCTOR: And you shot a blank with it.

DWIGHT: Doesn't matter, Corey fainted!

DOCTOR: Yes and he's had that coming for a long time. Anyone would agree.

SARAH: *(Enters.)* Dwight, what the hell is going on? Mike is freaking out. He said you brought a gun to school?!

DWIGHT: Sarah... I can't talk to you right now.

DOCTOR: There she goes again, sticking her face into your business—

DWIGHT: Shut up! *(To SARAH.)* I'm sorry, please, I'll explain later alright?

SARAH: Bullshit, you'll explain now!

DWIGHT: Sarah, I...I shot a blank at Corey.

SARAH: Are you insane?!

DWIGHT: Yes, I think I am.

SARAH: Why did you do that?

DWIGHT: I can't... You wouldn't get it. *(Sits on the couch.)*

SARAH: You don't know that unless you tell me.

DWIGHT: Because he said something about Susie. OK? I told you, you wouldn't understand.

SARAH: So explain it to me. *(Sits down next to him.)*

DWIGHT: I just want to be alone right now—

SARAH: No! I'm not letting you do this again! Dwight, sometimes you have to talk to someone.

DWIGHT: Why?

SARAH: Because if you don't, you go crazy.

Beat. DOCTOR stands and speaks for DWIGHT.

DOCTOR: I had a little sister named Susie. My mom was an alcoholic, so I had to take care of her most of the time. One time when I was eight, Susie wanted to go to the park and mom was passed out, so I took her... and...I still don't know exactly what happened. I was too young and I wasn't watching her closely enough and...she slipped into the river and drowned.

Beat. SARAH hugs him.

DWIGHT: I'm sorry I didn't tell you, I just—

SARAH: It's OK. You know that's not your fault though, right?

DOCTOR stands up and walks offstage. DWIGHT watches him go.

DWIGHT: …Yeah, I do.

SARAH: *(Kisses him.)* Good. So do you want to talk about it?

DWIGHT: Yeah, I do. But first we should go find Mike and tell him to calm down. *(They get up and start to leave.)*

SARAH: That's not going to be easy, he was really freaking out when I saw him.

DWIGHT: Well Mike's always been a little over dramatic. You know he cried when he saw *Free Willy*? *(They both laugh.)*

SARAH: Seriously though, you'll probably get expelled for this.

> *They exit together.*

> *The End.*

Letting Go

ROCHELLE FOUREE

"This play won third place in 2007. Rochelle, or Rocki, was our first finalist from Tec Voc High School in Winnipeg. Her teacher was so excited about Rocki's experience with us that he has encouraged his students to enter every year since. Tec Voc has become the most frequently represented school at our competition." —A.K.

Scene 1

> *Setting is a living room. MICHELLE is already on stage coloring. JASON enters and sees MICHELLE sitting on the couch. He walks up to her and flicks her ear. MICHELLE whines, and then JASON walks over to the television, turning it on as well as a video game.*

MICHELLE: Can I play?

JASON: *(Cold.)* Nope.

MICHELLE: *(Quietly.)* Nope.

> *JASON looks at her in disgust. Then, LINDA enters, followed by TOM.*

TOM: Well it's not like I have a choice here.

LINDA: I will not live here.

> *BOB enters.*

BOB: Why not? What's wrong with this place?

LINDA: Oh shut up. *(Turns to TOM.)* There's nothing to do here.

TOM: Well, we could use a little extra money, and you don't do anything all day.

LINDA: What are you suggesting? That I get a job? What the hell for?

BOB: I'll be needing rent money.

LINDA: Family shouldn't have to pay rent!

TOM: Mom's getting better Linda, the doctors say she's starting to eat all her meals, and she's getting her sense of humour back, c'mon.

LINDA: Yeah, yeah, yeah...I know what the doctors are saying...

BOB: C'mon, give baby boy a chance to be with his mama.

             LINDA turns to BOB.

LINDA: Do you mind?... God.

TOM: I want to see her well enough to come home, we can't leave now, I really think having us come up here to visit is the reason why she's getting better.

LINDA: What about the kids and school?

BOB: This town does have schools.

LINDA: *(To TOM.)* I'm about to kick the living shit out of him.

TOM: Honey, they can start school here.

JASON: What?!? I don't want to go the school here!

BOB: Just never mind you...watch some TV or something.

LINDA: I can't believe this...you're crazy you know! Sometimes I just wanna ...you know what, whatever, good luck negotiating it with the girls.

             LINDA angrily exits. TOM sighs.

BOB: Hmm, women.

TOM: Girls!

MELISSA: *(Heard offstage.)* What?

TOM: Get in here!

JESSICA: *(Heard offstage.)* We're busy.

TOM: Now!

                  *MELISSA and JESSICA enter while BOB exits. As he
                  is exiting, he checks out MELISSA, then he flicks her
                  pony tail. TOM is oblivious, JASON notices.*

MELISSA: *(To BOB.)* Get lost.

JESSICA: *(Sarcastically.)* Yes master.

TOM: Me and your mother have been talking and we agreed
                  that it would be best if we moved up here.

MELISSA/
JESSICA: What?!

MELISSA: You mean live here?

JESSICA: Why?

TOM: Because granny is getting better and I think having me
                  around is really good for her right now.

MELISSA: I can't live here, what about Mark?

JASON: Oh poor baby, what's the matter? Don't wanna live in
                  celibacy?

MELISSA: Shut up! *(To TOM.)* Why can't we go back while you
                  stay with her?

TOM: *(Now cranky.)* Because I said so alright! We're staying
                  here as a family, it's settled! It's final!

JESSICA: But…

TOM: Too bad! When you start paying the bills, you can
                  make decisions too, but until then, keep your mouth
                  shut and obey.

JASON stands up and faces TOM.

JASON: You only want us to stay here as a family because you're scared mom will leave us again!

JESSICA: *(Quietly.)* Jason.

JASON: Well it's true!

TOM: That's enough! I want us to stay here as a family because we never do anything together! Do you not like this family? You don't want to be a part of it? Then, leave!

JASON: Can't wait.

JASON turns to exit.

MELISSA: Jeez Jason, when will you ever learn to shut your mouth?

JASON: When will you ever learn to shut your legs?

JASON exits.

TOM: *(To JESSICA.)* Think of it as a new start...I promise.

MELISSA exits.

JESSICA: *(Sarcastically.)* Oh yes, another new start hooray.

MICHELLE lifts her hands in the air.

MICHELLE: Hooray!

JESSICA faintly smiles at MICHELLE, then exits, TOM sighs.

TOM: We can do it kiddo, we can do it.

Scene Two

Setting is a bedroom. JESSICA is sitting on the bed writing in her journal. MELISSA enters she is distressed.

JESSICA: What's wrong?

MELISSA: Everything.

JESSICA: Bad day at school?

MELISSA: Why didn't you wait for me?

JESSICA: 'Cause I had a spare.

MELISSA: Oh, right. I had the worst day.

JESSICA: What happened?

MELISSA: I went to the bathroom right after third period and on the side of the stall it said "Melissa Walton is a big fat whore!"

JESSICA: What?

MELISSA: I know! I bet you anything it was Ashley who wrote it! She's so immature, like really, who writes shit like that on the bathroom stall? You might as well be in junior high.

JESSICA: What's even more of a funny thought is what she was doing while she was writing it.

MELISSA: Ew.

> *They both laugh.*

JESSICA: Well, no offence, I'm not surprised. You did kind of kiss her boyfriend.

MELISSA: I didn't know they were going out! Besides he kissed me, and now he won't leave me alone.

JESSICA: You better pray you don't get accused of other things or you'll get your ass kicked.

MELISSA: Yeah.

> *Pause.*

JESSICA: Hey, guess what?

MELISSA:　Huh?

JESSICA:　I had a job interview on Tuesday.

MELISSA:　Really? Where?

JESSICA:　Food-town, it's for the cashier, or front person, whatever you want to call it.

MELISSA:　Jess, are you sure you want to get a job?

JESSICA:　Uh, yeah. I'm going to need a little extra money to go on my trip. Plus it gives me something to do.

MELISSA:　Wait, wait, what trip?

JESSICA:　I'm going back to the city, for Andrea's birthday.

MELISSA:　You sound determined. Are you sure Andrea's going to make time for you? She wont be too busy with her boyfriend?

JESSICA:　Of course she'll make time for me. It's not like we get to see each other everyday anymore.

MELISSA:　I hate to break it to you Jess, but the last time you got a job it didn't work out so well.

JESSICA:　I'm not even going to tell them.

MELISSA:　What if they find out?

JESSICA:　I'll fight them off.

MELISSA:　Last time you tried this, they bothered you all night and you ended up with empty pockets.

JESSICA:　Well, it's different this time. I know I can do it.

MELISSA:　Well, if you think you can do it, good luck.

Scene Three

> *LINDA is vegging on the couch and talking on the*
> *phone in the living room. She also has the remote*
> *control in her hand and the TV is blaring. MICHELLE*
> *is sitting on the floor playing with wooden blocks.*

LINDA: Was he mad that I didn't show up for my shift? *(Short pause.)* Oh well. *(Short pause.)* I don't know if I can go out tonight, I'll have to talk to my husband about it. I swear, ever since I took off that one Christmas he's been attached to my hip. *(Short pause.)* What's that? About…three months, but I don't know how long were going to stay, probably 'till the ol' bag dies.

MICHELLE: Mom look!

> *MICHELLE points to the tower of blocks. LINDA does*
> *not notice.*

Mom…mom…mommy look. Mom…

LINDA: Shh Michelle! I'm on the phone.

> *MICHELLE looks around the room. JESSICA enters.*

JESSICA: Hey Michelle that's really cool!

> *MICHELLE gives JESSICA a wide smile then turns*
> *back to her blocks*

MICHELLE: *(Quietly.)* Cool.

> *JESSICA sits down beside her mother.*

JESSICA: Mom?

> *LINDA waves her away.*

Mom I need to talk to you. It's important.

LINDA: *(Talking on the phone.)* Oh God…hang on a second, OK?

> *LINDA turns to JESSICA.*

LINDA: Can't you see I'm busy?

JESSICA: But it's really important

LINDA: This better be good. *(On phone.)* I'm going to have to let you go, damn kids. OK, bye.

                LINDA hangs up the phone.

JESSICA: I deserve to take a break and go to the city for the weekend.

LINDA: Why couldn't you wait 'till I got off the phone?

JESSICA: One you take too long, and two, I need to call someone to let them know that I'm going.

LINDA: Where on earth did you get money?

JESSICA: I got a job.

LINDA: You mean to tell me we're all starving here and you didn't have the decency to help us out? What makes you think I would let you go to the city? What makes you think your father would let you go to the city? I can't believe you Jess, I just—forget it, get out of my face. Go to your room or something…

                One of MICHELLE's blocks fall from the tower, she freaks out and starts to push the blocks around destroying the whole thing.

                Michelle, that is your last warning. Shut up!

                LINDA looks towards the TV. JESSICA walks over to MICHELLE.

MICHELLE: *(Whispering.)* I'm sorry Jessie.

JESSICA: *(Whispering.)* It's OK honey.

                The phone rings, LINDA answers it.

LINDA: Hello… What is it… I'll let the kids know. OK…yah… I love you too… Bye.

> *LINDA hangs up the phone and turns towards the TV.*

JESSICA: Who was that?

LINDA: Your dad

JESSICA: What did he say?

> *LINDA sighs.*

LINDA: Your grandma died this afternoon.

JESSICA: *(Gasps, then realize.)* What the hell is wrong with you? You just sit there and continue to watch TV? Just because you don't care doesn't mean we don't.

> *JESSICA angrily leaves the room.*

LINDA: Hey don't you ever talk to me like that again you little shit!

> *Black out.*

Scene Four

> *Scene is in JESSICA's room. MICHELLE enters, singing and humming to herself, she looks around the room and begins to jump on the bed. She then notices MELISSA's clothing on the floor, and starts to throw them around, laughing. Afterwards she begins to organize the clothes into pictures. MELISSA enters.*

MELISSA: Michelle!

> *MICHELLE turns towards her sister, frightened.*

(Raising her voice.) Oh my God! Why do you always do this? Get out of here!

> *MICHELLE stands still, staring at her sister.*

Go!

> *JESSICA enters. MICHELLE runs towards JESSICA*

and hides behind her, occasionally peeking from behind her.

JESSICA: Mel stop yelling at her, she doesn't understand that your pants are the most important thing in your life!

             JESSICA turns to MELISSA.

             Go play outside OK, and don't leave the yard.

             MICHELLE nods and exits.

MELISSA: I'm just sick and tired of her digging around in here, I don't know how many times I have to tell her not to touch things that aren't hers, I wish she would just stay...

JESSICA: ...In an institue? Just because she's a little different she should leave us and go live in some nut house? It seems like that's what everyone in this family seems to think.

MELISSA: I was going to say stay out of here.

JESSICA: So what if she likes making picture with clothes, she's got nothing else to do. We're all that she has.

             JESSICA sits on the bed.

MELISSA: I'm sorry. *(Short pause.)* I hate this place. Ashley has the whole school believing I'm some sort of tramp.

JESSICA: Yeah, I heard.

MELISSA: I wish we could go back home.

JESSICA: I guess he wasn't kidding when he said this was a new start.

             They both take a moment to re-collect their thoughts.

MELISSA: Well, I'm gonna go do laundry for Tommorow, you want anything washed?

JESSICA: No that's OK, you had a hard day, I'll do it before i go to work tonight.

MELISSA: OK.

                MELISSA exits. When JESSICA is sure that MELISSA
                is gone, she grabs her purse and pulls out some money.
                She puts the money in an envelope then putting the
                envelope in a box. She then puts the box in her top
                drawer. Then she exits.

                Black out.

Scene Five

                LINDA is sitting on the couch watching TV. BOB
                enters, talking on the phone.

BOB: Hey it's Bob here, over on Paul Ave., are you close?…
                Can you cuff me one? …In ten?… Alright.

                BOB hangs up the phone.

LINDA: Who's that?

BOB: Oh nothing. I was just askin' a buddy of mine to cuff
                me a rock.

                LINDA shows interest.

LINDA: Oh?

                LINDA thinks for a moment.

                What if…I could get some money? Do you think you
                could get me one?

BOB: Then I'd say when and where would you get it?

LINDA: Well, Jason just got a job thing doing flyers.

BOB: Ahh.

LINDA: Jason!

                JASON enters.

JASON: What?

LINDA: Lend me some money.

JASON: Yeah right away.

                JASON turns to exit.

LINDA: Jason.

JASON: Why?

LINDA: Just give it to me, never mind "why".

JASON: I'm not going to give you money for that shit!

BOB: Hey! Watch your mouth.

LINDA: Please son?

JASON: Why don't you ask Jess, she's got more than I do.

LINDA: She's out right now. Come on Jason.

                JASON takes a moment.

                Please?

JASON: Fine.

                JASON gives her a 20 dollar bill. Then storms off.

LINDA: Thank-you son.

                BOB picks up the phone, as he is dialing, TOM enters.

                We're gonna have a hoot, you want?

                TOM hesitates.

                I know you want it.

TOM: Where'd you get money?

LINDA: Jason lent me some.

                Pause.

                Well?

TOM: Yeah, sure.

BOB: *(On the phone.)* You're where?…

                BOB looks out the window.

                Oh. OK, I see you, go to the back and I'll be right out.

                BOB hangs up the phone, as he is exiting LINDA gives him the money. Then he exits.

                Pause.

TOM: Where is Jessica?

LINDA: I don't know, out.

                Pause.

TOM: When's she coming home?

LINDA: Beats the shit out of me.

                Pause, BOB enters.

BOB: You gotta pipe?

LINDA: Yeah. *(To TOM.)* Where is it?

                TOM exits. BOB grabs his pipe from his pocket. Then sits down, and puts a few pieces of rock in it. Then TOM enters, with his own pipe. BOB then pulls out a lighter, then lights it up. He passes the lighter to TOM, who does the same. TOM takes a few hoots then passes it to LINDA.

Scene Six

                After they are finished BOB and TOM are sitting on the couch while LINDA paces around the room.

LINDA: I need more… Tom, I need you to do me a favour.

TOM: What?

LINDA: Jessica has some cash somewhere in the room, go get it.

TOM: You do it.

LINDA: I don't wanna do it, I want you to do it.

TOM contemplates on whether he should go or not.

LINDA: Don't you want more?

TOM: I don't want to steal from her, I promised her…

LINDA: That never stopped you before.

BOB: Tom, stop being such a pussy, just go and get it.

LINDA: We are her parents, we feed her, we clothe her, we put a roof over her head. She owes us, and we deserve a break. I need more.

TOM just stands there.

Well, what are you waiting for? Go!

TOM exits.

Scene Seven

TOM is in JESSICA's room. He starts to look around her room, searching for the money. He then digs in her dresser drawer, he takes out a box and opens it, he finds the envelope with the money in it. He opens the envelope and pulls out some money half way, then puts it back in. As he is putting the envelope in his pocket MELISSA enters.

MELISSA: What are you doing?

TOM tries to hide his face from her. MELISSA walks right up to her father and hold his face in her hands.

Oh my God… Did you think you could fool us? You said you were going to stop, you said that moving here was a new start. You promised us! Where's mom? She's high too isn't she? Of course, when you get started you've gotta pull her into it.

TOM: Shh, calm down OK?

MELISSA: Don't you shush me! Get out, I can't even look at you right now.

> *TOM quietly exits. MELISSA sits on the bed and sobs.*

When is this going to end?

> *MELISSA calms down a little, then BOB enters.*

What do you want?

BOB: Where'd your dad go?

MELISSA: You had somthing to do with this didn't you? Who do you think you are? You knew they were trying to stop you asshole!

> *MELISSA stands up off the bed.*

BOB: Stop screaming, you shouldn't talk to your elders like that.

MELISSA: Is breaking up this family some sort of game to you? Why did you get them started?

BOB: I didn't get anybody started.

MELISSA: I bet your going to make them get more, because that's what you do! You get them started and then they want more and more, and then they waste their money on that shit instead of what we need in this house.

BOB: Jeez, stop spazzing, just let them have a little fun, they're grown adults they can get another one if they want. It's not like I'll be paying for it.

MELISSA: Well who is?

BOB: You should know your own parents by now, your

dad's so low, he went and stole your sister's money. I tried to stop him, but…

MELISSA: Shut up! I don't want to hear any more of this bullshit!

BOB: Well, what would you like to hear? Would you like to hear how you've grown into such a beautiful woman?

MELISSA: *(Oblivious.)* Fuck off Bob.

> *BOB starts to walk towards MELISSA.*

BOB: You're quite the fiesty one, that's what I love about you. You're so…

> *BOB starts to caress MELISSA arms.*

…Irresistible. Come on don't be so angry, would you like a hug? A hug from Uncle Bob?

> *BOB hugs her and kisses her neck, MELISSA tries to push him off.*

MELISSA: Stop it.

BOB: Don't fight it.

MELISSA: Get off of me!

> *MELISSA pushes him off.*

GET THE FUCK OUT!

BOB: Slut.

> *BOB exits.*

> *MELISSA sits on her bed, and quietly sobs to herself. Awhile later JESSICA enters with her work uniform on. MELISSA tries to hide her tears from JESSICA.*

JESSICA: What the hell is going on?!? I leave for a couple of hours and already they're at it again! For fuck sakes, when is his shit going to end?

JESSICA takes off her work apron, and puts on her regular apron. Then she notices MELISSA crying.

Melissa, what's wrong?

MELISSA: Nothing.

JESSICA: Well that's a pack of lies right there, c'mon…

JESSICA sits on the bed.

You can tell me anything.

MELISSA: Anything?

JESSICA: Anything.

MELISSA: Well, Bob told me, that, Dad took your trip money and spent it.

JESSICA: Are you sure?

MELISSA: Yes.

JESSICA: I knew he wouldn't keep his promises.

JESSICA turns and stares at MELISSA.

MELISSA: What?

MELISSA feels the pressure of JESSICA's stare.

It's, it's Bob.

JESSICA: What about him?

MELISSA: He tried to… *(Sighs.)* You cannot tell a soul Jessica. I mean it!

JESSICA: OK.

MELISSA: He was hitting on me.

JESSICA is astonished.

JESSICA: What do you mean? Did he touch you?

MELISSA: Well, he…

JESSICA: Did he touch you!?

             MELISSA starts to cry.

MELISSA: A little, he was holding me, and kissing me, and he wouldn't let go and I just—

             MELISSA cries more, JESSICA holds her.

             I hate it here. I don't want to live like this anymore.

JESSICA: Neither do I.

             JESSICA tries not to cry in front of MELISSA. MELISSA sits up and faces her sister.

MELISSA: Let's run away.

JESSICA: What?

MELISSA: C'mon, your next paycheck we could buy bus tickets to the city, and we could live with…uh…Grandpa.

JESSICA: Oh Melissa.

             JESSICA hugs MELISSA.

             We can't.

             MELISSA pulls away.

MELISSA: Why not?

JESSICA: We can't leave Jason and Michelle here, not by themsleves, and Michelle needs me. She wouldn't be able to carry out her routines if I wasn't here.

MELISSA: Well, what the hell are we supposed to do? I will not live here with that, that pig!

             JESSICA takes a moment to think.

JESSICA: How would you feel if I called…C.F.S.?

MELISSA: What is that, a foster home?

JESSICA: Yeah.

MELISSA almost jumps off the bed.

MELISSA: Are you crazy!? No, no you can't. I won't let you! No matter how bad things get you have to promise me that you won't call them.

JESSICA: If it's a better place to live why wouldn't you...

MELISSA: *(Interrupting.)* It's not a better place to live, we'd probably get split up, you talk about Michelle needing you, do you really think that this would be the best thing for her?

JESSICA stops to think.

Promise me you won't call!

JESSICA: *(Quietly.)* OK...I promise... So what's your plan of action if things get really bad. Not that they can get any worse.

MELISSA: We'll tough it out.

MELISSA holds her out her pinky finger.

We'll tough it out.

JESSICA: Yeah... OK...we'll tough it out.

JESSICA loops her pinky finger around MELISSA's, then they hug.

Scene Eight

MICHELLE is sitting on the couch watching TV and eating candy. JESSICA is cleaning up around the coffee table, she picks up a box of crayons and a bunch of paper that are lying on the ground.

MICHELLE: *(Whining.)* No, leave it.

JESSICA: OK.

JESSICA begins to walk to the other side of the room.

Do you want some juice?

MICHELLE: Yes please.

JESSICA exits. JASON enters. He then sees the candy that MICHELLE is eating, he takes the bag from MICHELLE.

Hey...no!

JASON starts to tease MICHELLE with the bag of candy.

Jason! Stop it! That's my candy, give it back, give it back to me!

JASON: Shut up!

MICHELLE begins to cry.

JESSICA: *(From offstage.)* What's going on?

MICHELLE continues to cry.

JASON: Nothing.

MICHELLE: *(Screaming.)* Give it to me!

JESSICA quickly enters, with a broom and a colorful cup of juice, MICHELLE's special cup.

JESSICA: What the hell is wrong with you? Dad's sleeping, he'll get pissed if you wake him up! Give her back her candy!

JASON: Well, it's not fair! How come she gets candy?

JESSICA: Because it keeps her quiet.

JASON: Whatever.

JASON throws the bag of candy at MICHELLE.

MICHELLE: Ow.

JESSICA: Jason!

                JASON stares at the TV.

                Now keep quiet.

                JESSICA hands MICHELLE her juice, then exits.
                JASON looks directly at MICHELLE, she looks back.

JASON: I hate you

                MICHELLE is oblivious to what he is saying.

                Everyone loves you, because you're so sweet and
                innocent, and everyone blames shit on me, because
                of you.

MICHELLE: *(Mimicking.)* Because of you.

JASON: God… Why don't you grow some fucking brains?

MICHELLE: That's a bad word.

                JASON hold up both middle fingers towards
                MICHELLE.

JASON: Fuck you!

                JASON exits.

Scene Nine

                JESSICA is napping on her bed. TOM enters, sits on
                the bed and watches his daughter sleep.

                He notices JESSICA's journal on the bed beside her. He
                picks it up, hesitates, then begins to read it. His facial
                expression turns from sympathetic to disgust as he
                reads more and more of the journal. JESSICA awakens
                and notices her journal missing from her arms, then
                she notices her dad reading her journal.

JESSICA: Hey, what are you doing?

TOM is startled by her, but ignores her and continues to read.

JESSICA: Hey! Gimme that!

JESSICA tries to grab her journal from TOM, but he moves it away so she can't reach it.

TOM: Is this what you think of me?

JESSICA: Give that to me, now.

TOM: It says...

TOM points to the journal.

"My dad is useless in all ways. He doesn't clean up, he doesn't look after Michelle, he doesn't work..."

TOM looks at JESSICA.

JESSICA: Why are you reading my journal?

TOM: Is this what you think? You think I'm a bad father? Do you know how hard it is to raise three teenagers and a half-brained retard?

JESSICA: Don't talk about her that way!

TOM: You think you're the person who holds this family together? I work my ass off to make sure you guys eat! Everything your mother does I get blamed for and...

JESSICA stands up, angry.

JESSICA: Bullshit! That's all you ever do, blame everything on everyone else, you asshole!

TOM throws down the journal, briskly walks up to JESSICA, grabs her arm, and motions to hit her.

TOM: Listen you little shit... Don't you ever talk to me like that again.

MICHELLE enters with a picture in her hand.

MICHELLE: Look Jessie!

TOM: Not now.

MICHELLE: Jessie, look!

TOM: I said not now!

               TOM walks up to MICHELLE, grabs her, and spanks her.

JESSICA: Hey!

               MICHELLE starts to cry.

TOM: Shut up, I do the disciplining around here.

JESSICA: No you don't, I do! You're never around, and when you are you're either high, or you just don't seem to care.

               MICHELLE begins to cry louder. JESSICA begins to yell.

               I raise this family, not you, or mom. If I wasn't here you'd be nowhere, because instead of spending your money on groceries, you'd be spending it on crack... *(Short pause.)* I am the person who holds this family together.

               MICHELLE covers her ears and starts screaming.

MICHELLE: STOP YELLING! STOP YELLING!

TOM: You wanna cry? You wanna cry? I'll give you something to cry about.

               TOM backhands MICHELLE several times.

JESSICA: *(Screams.)* Dad, Dad! Get off of her!

               TOM lets go of MICHELLE, and goes to hit JESSICA.

MICHELLE: *(Screams.)* No, Daddy stop!

> *Everything pauses. MICHELLE's quiet crying is heard.*

No, Daddy stop…

> *TOM lets go of JESSICA, and exits. JESSICA starts to cry, MICHELLE crawls to JESSICA. They hold each other crying together.*

JESSICA: It's OK Michelle, it's OK… You're safe now, Jessica's here, things will get better. Do you wanna watch a movie?

MICHELLE: OK…

JESSICA: OK, well go in the other room, and I'll be there in a few minutes alright?

> *MICHELLE exits, still wiping her tears. JESSICA sits on the bed holding her head in her hands. MELISSA enters.*

MELISSA: What's going on? Are you OK?

JESSICA: You have to let me phone, please let me phone…

MELISSA: No! You promised! No matter how bad things get, you made a promise to me, and now you have to tough things out, just like I would.

JESSICA: Let me phone…

MELISSA: Stop trying to be the hero, you're not our mom Jessica, you don't need to take care of us.

JESSICA: We can't stay here, I won't let you guys stay in this house. Not with those three. If we stay here so many things will go wrong, Jason will end up in a gang, I know it, Dad can't control himself anymore and mom doesn't give a shit about us. Do you feel safe after what Bob did to you? What would stop him from going after Michelle?

MELISSA: My life is already shitty, I'm not going to make it worse. I already have to deal with living in this shit hole, and school, I don't need the whole town knowing that the Walton kids are in C.F.S.!

JESSICA smirks.

JESSICA: Just like mom…

MELISSA: What did you say?

JESSICA: I said you're just like…

MELISSA: Don't you dare say mom! I am not like her, I—

JESSICA: Yes you are, all you ever care about is what other people think about you. You only think for yourself, and you always leave me in the dust, you think your life is shitty? Try living in my shoes.

MELISSA: So in reality, the only reason why you want to phone is so that *your* life isn't shitty anymore.

JESSICA: What? No—

MELISSA: You are such a selfish bitch! You seem to think you're the only one putting money into the house and holding us together but your not.

JESSICA: Melissa, you and I both know that. I do way more around here than…

MELISSA: *(Interrupting.)* You help, but I'm sure we'd be fine without you. You *think* you're the person who keeps us together but like I said you're not.

JESSICA: How would you know? You were never around, you were always out with your friends, while I was at home cooking and cleaning and doing what Linda was supposed to be doing. Ever since Michelle came into this world I haven't had a childhood. I *am* the person who holds us together I know because you always come to me for comfort and support, not them.

MELISSA: You're not going to call. You made a promise to me, you promised that you'd tough it out! If you break that promise then you'd be just like dad! Now TOUGH IT OUT!

MELISSA makes JESSICA pinky swear. They hug. MELISSA exits. JESSICA is left standing with her pinky in the air, she cries to herself. Then drops her pinky finger.

JESSICA: I can't do this anymore. But, I can't break my promise and be like him.

JESSICA reaches for the phone and hesitates.

Oh…what do I do?

JESSICA takes the phone and begins to dial, but then quickly hangs up. After contemplating, she picks up the phone and dials, letting it ring. JESSICA takes a deep breath.

Oh God, it's ringing

JESSICA hangs up again. She takes a moment to think.

This is for you Michelle.

JESSICA takes off her apron, and throws it to the ground angrily, she then picks the phone and dials letting it ring.

Oh hurry up before I change my mind…

Short pause.

Uh…hello…I need some help.

The End.

Perspective

Maria Funk

"This play, from Tec Voc High School, won third place in 2007. Stylistically, it shared some of the stark realism of (fellow Tec Voc student) Rocki's play. In terms of subject matter, it explored some familiar territory in a totally unique way." —A.K.

Scene One, Opening

	The play is set in a hospital room, with a bed for ANYA and one or two chairs for others to use as needed. The set should be small and sterile, preferably without decorations of any kind. ANYA enters in a wheelchair with DAD and JERRY.
ANYA:	*(Is young and self-assured.)* You know, I don't need a wheelchair. I can walk just fine by myself.
DAD:	*(Is quiet, calm, and competent.)* I know, but it's best if you just rest. You gave us a pretty good scare, you know.
ANYA:	I just got knocked out for a bit in gym, all this isn't necessary. I probably got hit in the head with a basketball, or something. Really, I don't need to stay in the hospital.
JERRY:	*(Acts bratty, but slightly idolizes ANYA.)* Yeah, sure you were hit in the head. That's why no one could wake you up until we got to the waiting room.
DAD:	The doctors said you had a pretty advanced case of dehydration, but there was no cause for it. They're just holding you over the weekend to make sure that nothing serious is wrong with you.

ANYA: Yeah, I know. *(Looks around.)* What's taking Mom so long?

JERRY: I don't know, I'll go look for her.

DAD: Remember the room number so you can tell your Mom.

ANYA: And so you won't get lost!

JERRY: Shut up. *(Exits.)*

ANYA: *(Sighs.)* This is going to suck. Will you make sure to tape my shows for me?

DAD: Sure. I didn't know kids now still used the term 'taping shows'. I thought it was all about 'burning' now.

ANYA: You know what I mean. Besides, Mom is too cheap to agree to get a DVD burner.

DAD: Well, that cheapness is what keeps us getting by, and keeps you fed. If you can call it food…

ANYA: I know. I can't wait for breakfast at the hospital cafeteria; I'll finally get to eat something good!

DAD: *(Laughs.)* That isn't very nice.

ANYA: Yeah, but neither is Mom's cooking.

DAD: Just don't let her hear that.

MOM: *(Enters with JERRY.)* Let 'her' hear what?

ANYA: Nothing, Dad was just making jokes at your expense again.

DAD: Sure I was. Here, let me help you. *(Mimes throwing ANYA onto the bed, but then actually helps her onto the bed carefully.)*

MOM: *(A worrywart who likes things to always go her way, but she is also a very a kind person.)* Oh, be careful, don't hurt yourself! Watch that sharp edge! Honestly, why do they have such a dangerous bed in a hospital at all? Some poor person might hurt themselves even more badly on something like that. I'll have to talk to the doctor about this. Give me a moment, I'll be right back. *(Exits.)*

JERRY: Mom thinks that doctor knows everything.

ANYA: Maybe you should be a doctor. Then she might finally listen to you.

JERRY: Oh shut up!

DAD: Hey, play nice or I'll separate you two.

JERRY: We're just fooling around, Dad.

ANYA: Yeah, you know he isn't smart enough to be a doctor, and the only thing I'm good at is running.

DAD: Which reminds me, I'm going to have to call your coach and tell him that you won't be at Track practice tomorrow.

ANYA: Aw Dad, you don't have to do that. After some sleep and some good hospital food in the morning, I'll be ready to run again by noon!

JERRY: 'Good' hospital food... How does that work?

ANYA: It doesn't.

DAD: Except when it's better than your Mom's. *(Laughter, small chuckles.)*

MOM: *(Enters and bustles around, reluctant to leave.)* The doctor told me that he'd do his best to get you a newer, safer bed, but you really need to rest, and I'm pretty sure the meter is going to run out soon. I'll be back as soon as I can, so don't you worry. You'll be out of here in no time.

ANYA: Alright. Love you Mom.

MOM: *(Hugs ANYA tightly.)* Sleep well sweetheart, I love you too.

DAD: I could stay with you for a bit. Help you get settled in.

MOM: Oh darling, I'm sure she'll be fine on her own, won't you sweetheart? Or do you want us to stay?

ANYA: Mom, Dad, I'm a big girl! I can handle staying by myself in the big, scary hospital.

JERRY: Yeah, she's not even scared of the dark anymore.

ANYA: Shut up.

MOM: Well, if you're sure…

ANYA: I'll be fine.

DAD: Alright, alright, the big girl stays on her own. We'll see you in a bit, OK?

ANYA: OK. Love you, Dad.

JERRY: *(From the door.)* See ya.

ANYA: Bye.

> *MOM, DAD, JERRY exit.*

This isn't so bad. It's pretty quiet, and this bed isn't too uncomfortable. Eh, I'll be fine. *(Settles in, yawns.)* I'll be out of here in no time.

Scene Two, Time Passes

> *A few personal effects should be added to the room and it should have a less sterile feel to it now. The scene begins with ANYA sleeping in a different position than she fell asleep in during the previous scene. MOM enters carrying a covered dish and wakes ANYA.*

MOM: Good morning sweetheart, rise and shine! You've been in this room for far too long. It's a beautiful new day, and I brought you your breakfast. I know no one really likes hospital food, so I brought it from home. If you eat it quickly, it should still be warm.

ANYA: Thanks Mom, but I'm not really hungry. I'll eat it later.

MOM: Are you sure? The doctor said you need to eat to keep up your strength. And then you can go home while the tests are being processed. Wouldn't you like that?

ANYA: I guess so. I'm tired of being stuck here.

MOM: Really? Well then, I'll talk to that smart young doctor about having you moved to a nicer room.

ANYA: What? No, that's alright Mom. *(Very sarcastic.)* I like this room, and I'm already settled in *so* nicely.

MOM: *(Misses the sarcasm.)* Well, if you're sure... But I don't know about that. I'll still talk to the doctor and be certain. I want my baby to be comfortable.

ANYA: I'd be more comfortable if I were at home.

MOM: Oh sweetheart, you know that you can't come home yet. It's not your fault, it's just waiting on these tests.

ANYA: *(Fed up.)* Mom, could you get me that glass of water? I'm a little thirsty now.

MOM: Oh, certainly. Why don't you have a table nearby for that? I'm really going to have to talk to the doctor about this. You need to be comfortable while you're here.

ANYA: Are you joking? How *could* I be comfortable here? In this place? The smell of disinfectant is so strong it makes me want to gag. They seem to wash my clothes in bleach and starch, and the orderlies treat me like crap. At least I'm out of the way over here, or things would probably be worse. Mom, why am I being punished for getting sick?

MOM: *(Uncertain.)* I'm sure you're being silly. Maybe this room isn't all that comfortable, but you're just making a mountain out of a molehill. I'll talk to the doctor

. about it, I promise. Now here, sweetheart, let me help you with your straw.

ANYA: Mum, I'm not an invalid. I can sit up on my own to drink. The doctor only said-

MOM: Oh, I know what the doctor said; you don't have to tell me. He told you not to move around too much, I remember. That's why you're going to use the straw.

ANYA: Aw, Mom...

MOM: Here, sip slowly. I'll talk to the doctor in a little bit, and tell him about getting you a different room. I'm sure he'll look into getting you a transfer, but it might take a while. The hospital is very full, you know.

ANYA: Mum, I don't really want-

MOM: I read in the newspaper just the other day that all the hospitals seem to be short-staffed lately. And if you just look around this place, you can see that it's true. Oh! I just remembered they're having a musician of some kind performing in the lounge by the elevator right about now. Let's go watch!

ANYA: Mum, I can't go, you just said—

MOM: Oh sweetheart, it'll be good for you to get out for a little while. *(Helps ANYA into a wheelchair.)* You like music after all. I don't see a problem. And you won't really be moving all that much, because I'll be pushing you in the wheelchair. Come on sweetheart, let's go. It'll take your mind off things.

ANYA: *(Sighs and gives up.)* Alright Mom, lets go see what's playing. *(Lighthearted.)* Maybe they'll play some hard rock, and get all of the paraplegics head banging!

MOM: *(Misses the joke entirely.)* Oh I should certainly hope not!

          Both exit.

Scene Three, Darkening

> *ANYA wheels herself in alone on her wheelchair. She gets to the side of the bed and struggles to walk two steps required to get onto it. Frustrated, ANYA tries to move too quickly and nearly falls over, only saving herself by grabbing onto the edge of the bed just in time. Pulling herself carefully upright, ANYA is trembling with exhaustion and is out of breath. Disgusted, she kicks the wheelchair and tries to pull back the covers. JERRY enters.*

JERRY: Hey, what's up?

ANYA: *(Trying to hide her panting.)* Nothing.

JERRY: Do you want a hand?

ANYA: No!

JERRY: Well, sorry! I was just trying to help.

ANYA: *(Pauses, then finally pull back the covers.)* No, I'm sorry. It's just…

JERRY: Why can't you breathe?

ANYA: *(Getting into bed.)* It's just the doctor! He keeps going on and on about how I'll get to go home in a few days. Even though it's what I've been waiting for, I'm starting to not look forward to it at all!

> *ANYA settles in and pulls the covers over her legs. JERRY feels more comfortable and moves closer.*

JERRY: I know, Mum's just like that at home. She has it on the calendar, and every morning, it's like; "Oh, only five more days!" "Only four more days!" God, it's driving me nuts. It's all she talks about. I mean, it's not that I don't want you to come home, just…

ANYA: Nah, I get it. *(Bitter.)* Anyway, don't worry about it. With my luck I'll only be home for a few days before I'm right back here again.

JERRY: No way. You'll be coming home to stay.

ANYA: *(Changing the subject.)* You haven't been in to see me much lately.

JERRY: *(Evasive.)* I've been busy with some of my new friends, sorry.

ANYA: S'OK. What are they like?

JERRY: They're OK, I guess. Mum and Dad don't like them.

ANYA: Oh, those kinds of friends, huh?

JERRY: I guess so…

ANYA: Then, how are things at school?

JERRY: Everyone's been asking where you are, and what's happened to you. There're tons of stories running around, and every time I tell someone that Mom and Dad haven't buried your body in the backyard, I hear someone else talking about how you ran away from home.

ANYA: That's so stupid.

JERRY: I know! You'll have to straighten them out when you get back to school.

ANYA: Yeah…

JERRY: 'Cause you're coming back to school when you're better, right?

ANYA: When I get better…

JERRY: I mean, you want your diploma.

ANYA: Yeah, I guess so.

JERRY: You *guess* so?

ANYA: When I get better.

JERRY: You *are* going to get better.

ANYA: I guess you're right.

JERRY: The doctors just have to figure out what's wrong with
             you. It won't be long before you're back at home,
             where you belong.

ANYA: It shouldn't take very long at all.

Scene Four, Grey

                *MOM stands in the hallway outside ANYA's room,
                looking shell shocked. DAD approaches from offstage.*

DAD: Honey? Are you alright?

MOM: *(Whispering.)* Oh darling...

DAD: *(Goes to MOM.)* Honey, tell me what's wrong?

MOM: The doctor just told me...the new tests came back...

DAD: *(Fearing the worst.)* What is it?

MOM: *(Slowly growing more and more panicked.)* They're all
             inconclusive. Again. They have no idea what's wrong!
             And if they don't know what's wrong, how in the
             world can they fix it? What will happen if they can't
             fix it?!

DAD: Honey, calm down. You mean all the tests have come
             back inconclusive *again*? All of them?

MOM: Yes. Oh God. Darling, what do we do?

DAD: I...I have to talk to the doctor about this. Give me a
             minute.

MOM: *(Close to tears.)* Alright. Please hurry.

                DAD exits offstage.

             How can this be happening? How can this happen to
             my baby? Why did it have to be her? It's so far before
             her time. What's happening to her? Why can't I do
             anything to stop it?!

> *MOM pulls herself together and enters the room. She flutters around frantically, trying to keep herself busy. Through the following dialogue ANYA is only apathetic or tired.*

Hello sweetheart, how are you? Would you like me to fluff your pillow for you?

ANYA: No, that's fine Mom.

MOM: How about a glass of water? I'll bet you're parched! You always are. You'd think those nurses would do something about that. They are overworked, I know, but really, you'd think that they would at least get you a glass of water.

ANYA: No, it's fine. I'm fine. Or at least, as fine as I can be, all things considered.

MOM: Your brother... Your brother showed me those pictures you drew while you were waiting for the tests to come back. He said you drew them after you saw your school friends again.

ANYA: Yes. He promised he would burn them.

MOM: Oh, well, thank heavens then! I was worried I'd have to take them out in the middle of the night and burn them myself! What your father would say to that, I really wonder...

ANYA: I don't know.

MOM: Yes, well, who knows what that man thinks about anything? He's always off in his own little world, even when he's talking to someone seriously.

ANYA: Dad just thinks a lot.

MOM: Oh yes, I know, I know. I love that man dearly, but he's just too much at times. Just the other day, we were planning this trip here to see you, and he's just sitting there and staring at the newspaper. I could tell he wasn't reading it though, he never really does anymore. And then, I said; "*And what have I just told you?!"* because I was angry that he wasn't listening to me. And then do you know what he said to me?

ANYA: Everything that you'd just told him.

MOM: *(Startled.)* How did you know?

ANYA: *(Shrugs.)* That's just how Dad is.

MOM: Oh yes, of course. You're right, of course. So, is there anything you need? I'll get you your glass of water.

ANYA: Mom.

MOM: Huh? Oh that's right, you said you didn't need one. Still, you might need one in a little while, so I might as well get for you now. I want to talk to you without interruptions!

ANYA: You haven't let me get a word in edgewise.

MOM: I have so sweetheart! You're imagining things.

ANYA: You haven't let me do anything other than agree with you. I have some things I have to talk to you about. Please, just sit down.

MOM: Oh alright, if it'll make you feel better. *(Sits.)* What is it?

ANYA: Stop worrying about me.

MOM: What? How can I stop worrying about you?! You're here, like this! My baby is in pain, I can't do anything, and you don't want me to worry? How can you say something like that!

ANYA: You're the one who's in pain, and you're driving everyone else over the edge because of it! The world isn't going to end just because I'm gone.

MOM: But *my* world will. *(Pause.)*

ANYA: Mum, I'm just one person. One. There are other people who need you. I'm not that important. The most I could've ever done with my life is run.

MOM:	You were a great runner!
ANYA:	I was. But that wouldn't really change anything. I wasn't good enough to go pro. It was nothing. Really, in the end, I didn't matter. In the grand scheme of things, I don't matter.
MOM:	How can you say that?
ANYA:	Because I'm dying... It gives you a lot of time to think.
MOM:	*(Very uncomfortable.)* How did you... You shouldn't be talking like this!
ANYA:	Does this scare you Mom? I'm sorry. Maybe I should talk to Dad about this instead. He isn't as squeamish as you are.
MOM:	*(Jumps up.)* Your drugs must be making you act like this! I'll have to tell the doctor, and he'll do something to fix it. I'm sorry sweetheart, I can't believe I didn't realize sooner; I'll be back in just a bit. Don't you worry; Mommy will make it all better. *(Exits.)*
ANYA:	You... None of you understand. But then, I guess none of you have died before. It's just so strange, to know that this is the end. That all that hope and praying and wishing ended up meaning nothing. And I still don't even know what's killing me. Ha! Now that's funny.

Scene Five, Black

ANYA:	Things shouldn't have to end like this. I should be... well, not here! *(Speaking to the air.)* You are a sick son of a bitch, you know that? A measly forty four days of freedom. A month and a half away from here! And then you send me back. I may not have been the best person in the world, but I don't deserve this! Nobody deserves this living hell! Day after day, hour after hour staring at this stupid ceiling and waiting to die in a pointless little cube! Hell isn't fire and brimstone! Hell is off-white walls and nurses who won't even

give you a glass of water and having to suffer through sponge baths and getting someone to hold you while you pee! And the doctors! The damn doctors who keep telling you to hope, even though after so long you know there isn't any hope left. This place is Hell. *(ANYA contemplates the plug in the wall keeping her alive, or equivalent.)*

I don't want this anymore. I don't want this pathetic half-life. I got to go home and see everyone again, but the way they looked at me... Like I was some helpless little half-dead *thing*... I can't go back now. I can't go back and I can't stand to be here, so all I've got is the future. However long that is. Maybe... Maybe I should just end it now, on my terms. Take away the hard choice for them, while I still can. *(ANYA tries to lean over to reach the plug with a determined look. It appears as though she is actually going to do it, when she stops and breaks down.)*

God help me. Please God, help me. Allah, Buddha, anybody! Someone please, help me. *(Weakly.)* I don't want to die. There's so much I haven't done yet. I haven't even had my first real kiss. I haven't even gone on a real first date. I haven't gone to a bar, or made bad choices, or even been a real grown up yet. I don't want to die. Not when I haven't even lived yet... *(ANYA stares at the plug again.)*

But this is the end. I know it. I'm never going to leave this Hell ever again. I don't know what to do. *(Looks up.)* You can't help me. No one can. If I had another chance... Someone please, help me...

Lights down.

Scene Six, Ending the Story

DAD enters. He is calm now, but worn and tired looking. ANYA is exhausted, frail, and partly distracted.

DAD:　　　　　How are you holding out?

ANYA: Hey Dad. The drugs help a lot. I don't know what I'd do without them.

DAD: Yeah.

ANYA: How's Mom doing?

DAD: She doesn't like going near your room. But she wants to get rid of those drawings of yours.

ANYA: She doesn't like the blood?

DAD: I don't like it either. Where did you get that blood from anyway?

ANYA: Didn't you notice? The blood was layered. I would just pick my skin off and rub the blood on. It built up slowly after a couple of days. I thought you would notice.

DAD: You put your own blood on drawings of dead bodies while you were in the hospital. I didn't really want to look at them, all things considered.

ANYA: I just couldn't stand the way my friends looked at me when they saw me. Like I was already dead. I just picked up a pen and…the drawings came out.

DAD: I suppose something like that is understandable. It's tough.

ANYA: I didn't even think that something like this could actually happen in real life.

DAD: Yeah, young and headstrong. You never think it could happen to you.

ANYA: I guess not. Looking back, all the stuff I didn't notice, it seems obvious that it would end like this, doesn't it?

DAD: *(Sighs and changes the subject.)* Your Mom's been crying a lot at night.

ANYA: She has?

DAD: Yeah. I get home and I can hear her sobbing her heart out upstairs.

ANYA: Poor Mom…

DAD: She stops and pretends to be asleep when I go up to bed, but we both know I hear.

ANYA: She needs you.

DAD: I think I need her more. *(Pause.)* Jerry has been spending a lot of time over at his new friends' houses.

ANYA: Is it me, or Mom?

DAD: Both, I think. They're not good kids he's hanging out with either. It worries me.

ANYA: Jerry's a smart kid. He'll be OK.

DAD: I wonder…

ANYA: Are they that bad?

DAD: They might be involved in some less than legal stuff, but I don't want to yell at your brother when things are like this.

ANYA: …'Like this,' huh…?

DAD: …Yeah… *(Pause.)*

ANYA: Dad?

DAD: Yeah?

ANYA: I…I don't think I want to die.

DAD: I don't want that to happen to you either. None of us do. But…there's nothing we can do now but hope, and pray.

ANYA: I know…I know! That's why I hate this! I hate myself for getting sick in the first place. I hate Mom for trying to ignore it and act like nothing's wrong. I hate that there's nothing anyone can do to stop it! I wish…

DAD: I know.

ANYA: How? How can you know what it's like to die?

DAD: Your grandpa and grandma are dead. Do you think
            I've never had to deal with death before?

ANYA: ...I didn't think...

DAD: I've noticed.

ANYA: But you...and Mom...

DAD: We're dealing with this. It's difficult.

ANYA: Difficult to watch your kid waste away? Suffer? Die?

DAD: Yeah. And it only gets harder. Things like this, they're
            hard. But, in time, it's just something that has to
            happen. You can't run away from it.

ANYA: ...Dad?

DAD: Yeah?

ANYA: I, uh... Thanks for visiting me today. I'm a little tired
            now. Sorry.

DAD: Don't be sorry. Get some rest. I'll be here when you
            wake up.

ANYA: Yeah OK... But...

DAD: Yeah?

ANYA: I, uh... I'm sorry, about what I said.

DAD: Don't be. Right now, everything is forgiven.

ANYA: (Tries to make a joke.) Even that time I accidentally
            dropped your birthday cake, and it splattered all over
            the floor? It got all over your nice work shoes.

DAD: Yeah, even that.

ANYA: Thanks.

DAD: No problem. That's what I'm here for.

ANYA: When I die...don't forget me, OK? But, I want you guys to remember me before this happened. I don't want you to forget the way I used to be.

DAD: I won't. I know Jerry and your Mom won't.

ANYA: Thanks, Dad. I... I love you, you know that?

DAD: Yeah. I love you too.

ANYA: Thanks Dad.

DAD: Now, you get some sleep.

ANYA: Uh, one last thing?

DAD: Yeah?

ANYA: When I die...could you...ah, well, could you put my ashes in that pond we used to go fishing in? The one with that huge old tree, and that giant fish we could never catch? The one that ate, like, 15 of our lures?

DAD: Sure. Yeah, I could do that. Though, I think the last count was thirteen and a half.

ANYA: Right, the pink sparkly one. I really liked that one.

DAD: I remember. Since you're nodding off, I'll just shut my eyes for a bit too. Is that alright?

ANYA: That sounds fine. I love you Dad.

DAD: Love you too. *(Falls asleep.)*

ANYA: Bye.

          Blackout.

          The End.

Death (And Other Small Issues of Communication)

Jessy Ardern

"This play came in third in 2008, which was Jessy's second time as a finalist in this competition. Previously, she had submitted a more serious play, into which she had poured her heart and soul—and it had not been selected as a finalist. She confessed to having been shocked when this one, which she had simply written quickly, to amuse herself, was selected. This play is proof that sometimes a writer's best work happens when she is having fun." —A.K.

> *ELIZABETH is sitting outside beside an open coffin. We cannot see into it; there was a problem with the equipment and the funeral has halted. Everyone else has gone inside to eat mini sandwiches and talk in lowered tones. ELIZABETH is wearing businesslike but slightly soiled funeral attire and is drinking a martini. An empty glass sits at her feet. Lights show that it is a pleasant day outside. Sombre funeral music plays loudly and is suddenly cut off by ELIZABETH…*

ELIZABETH: Fuck. *(No response—hopefully the audience will think she is delivering a monologue.)* You know, I have four clients to call today. I don't have time for this.

IAN: *(From inside the coffin.)* Oh really. Sorry to inconvenience you.

ELIZABETH: Well, pardon me for breathing.

IAN: Just don't take it for granted.

ELIZABETH: Listen, asshole, being dead doesn't make you wise, OK?

IAN: For God's sake, Elizabeth *(Sitting up so that the audience can see him.)* there's a nice cozy funeral home for you to go drink in. This is a resting place.

ELIZABETH: And as soon as you're resting in the ground, I'll leave. But until then, I'm going to sit right here.

IAN: Even when I'm dead you won't leave me alone!

ELIZABETH: Hey, I didn't ask for this. Believe me, I have better things to do than wait around for someone to fix a bunch of damn equipment.

IAN: Well, could you wait somewhere else? Like in the reception, where all the other booze-guzzlers are?

ELIZABETH: I am not going in there. Aunt Marge is in there.

IAN: You deserve Aunt Marge.

ELIZABETH: You deserve death.

IAN: Bite me.

ELIZABETH: I don't want to get worms.

IAN: Well, looks like we're both getting what we deserve. *(He settles back into the coffin.)*

Enter AUNT MARGE wearing a large hat.

MARGE: Oh Lizzie! Oh, Oh Lizzie, it's so terrible. *(AUNT MARGE hugs ELIZABETH, and ELIZABETH finds her head shoved in AUNT MARGE's bosom.)* Oh, Lizzie, dear, you must feel so…so…distraught! Ian was such a wonderful man…such a great…great…

ELIZABETH: Big moron?

IAN: *(Popping back up into view.)* Elizabeth, shut up.

MARGE: A great person. *(She releases ELIZABETH's head.)*

IAN: At least someone appreciates me.

ELIZABETH: Piss off, Ian.

MARGE: Imagine! A heart attack! Who would have ever

expected it? And so young! I didn't think it would ever happen!

ELIZABETH: He was probably doing lots of cocaine or something.

IAN: Cocaine? What are talking about?! Just 'cause I'm dead doesn't mean I can't hear you.

MARGE: Cocaine, dear? They said it was a condition!

IAN: Yeah, an undiagnosed condition.

ELIZABETH: For God's sake, Ian, I was kidding. You're worse than she is.

MARGE: You look distracted, dear.

ELIZABETH: I keep hearing Ian's voice in my head.

IAN: Oh, Christ, now she'll think you're a kindred spirit and keep inviting you over for tea.

MARGE: That's only natural, dear. He's only been gone a few days...your mind will certainly be going over the precious moments you spent together.

IAN: Elizabeth, did you let your cousin fix your hair again? It looks like shit.

MARGE: The first time you met...

ELIZABETH: (To IAN.) Worst day of my life.

MARGE: The giddiness of young love, the first time you kissed, the day he asked you to marry him, that first night of wedded bliss when he—

IAN: Stop her Lizzie, STOP HER! (ELIZABETH starts to cough loudly and not unconvincingly.)

MARGE: Of course, you must also be feeling bad about those last few months of tension, but it's important to focus on the good things, dear! The good things.

IAN: Hah!

ELIZABETH: Aunt Marge, wouldn't you be more comfortable waiting with everyone else inside?

MARGE: I just couldn't bear the thought of you crying out here all alone, so I...is that a martini, dear? I didn't know they served those.

ELIZABETH: There's more inside the funeral home, Aunt Marge. Go get one for yourself, they're delicious.

IAN: I do not want her getting drunk and singing "Danny Boy" as I'm lowered into the ground.

ELIZABETH: And I don't want to sit here reminiscing with her.

MARGE: I really shouldn't leave you here, dear. What if you start to have... *(Whispering.)* suicidal thoughts?

ELIZABETH: I really think I'll be fine. *(AUNT MARGE hesitates.)* If I start feeling depressed, I'll do those deep breathing exercises you taught me, alright?

MARGE: Good idea, dear. *(She starts inhaling and exhaling loudly, reminding ELIZABETH about how do them.)* Whooooo... Haaa...

ELIZABETH: Yeah, yeah... Whooo...haaa... Go find yourself some liquor.

MARGE: I'll be right back to aid you in your grievance. *(She exits.)*

IAN: Grievance.

ELIZABETH: She meant grief, idiot.

IAN: I'm the idiot? You haven't changed a bit, have you.

ELIZABETH: Oh, I don't need to change. And do you know why? Because the only thing that was wrong with me before was being married to you. And now, you're dead. And if they ever manage to find the equipment or the person or whatever the hell we've been waiting for in order to bury you, I'm going to dance on your grave, spit, and leave. And then, I'll be perfect.

IAN: Fine!

ELIZABETH: Fine!

IAN: Fine! I'll just lie here… and be dead. *(He lies back down.)*

ELIZABETH: Fine. *(She slugs down the remainder of her martini. There is a pause.)*

IAN: *(Muttering.)* Lush.

ELIZABETH: Ass.

IAN: Boozehound.

ELIZABETH: Vindictive twerp.

IAN: Alcoholic.

ELIZABETH: Workaholic.

IAN: *(Popping back up.)* I was not!

ELIZABETH: No, not until that little secretary of yours came waltzing in.

IAN: Always with the affair!

ELIZABETH: Yes, always with the affair! It's a big deal!

IAN: I really don't see why.

ELIZABETH: You slept with another woman!

IAN: It happened once!

ELIZABETH: She was your secretary! I mean, how clichéd is that? Your secretary! And her name was Cindy! Cindy! Oh my fucking God.

IAN: What's wrong with Cindy?

ELIZABETH: Nothing, if you want to sleep with a perfect stereotype of a home-wrecking whore.

IAN: She is not a stereotype.

ELIZABETH: She was blonde!

IAN: And she is not a whore!

ELIZABETH: I don't care if she was the flying fucking nun before she met you, she's a whore now!

IAN: Elizabeth, we had split up!

ELIZABETH: For five days!

IAN: Oh I'm sorry, next time I'll wait a week.

ELIZABETH: There is no next time, genius. You're dead.

IAN: Yeah, well you're crazy.

ELIZABETH: I am not crazy.

IAN: Yes you are.

ELIZABETH: No I'm not!

IAN: Are so.

ELIZABETH: Am not!

IAN: Are so. (*He lies back down.*)

ELIZABETH: I am not crazy, you stupid dead person!

Enter AUNT MARGE with two fresh drinks.

MARGE: Ooh, there's the distraughtedness coming through, dear. I brought you one of those cute umbrella drinks.

ELIZABETH: When are they putting this thing in the ground?

MARGE: As soon as they can, dear. Now, tell me. How are you feeling?

ELIZABETH: I want him in the ground.

MARGE: Yes, dear, that's perfectly natural.

ELIZABETH: I want him buried. I want him six feet under. No, ten feet under.

MARGE: Yes, dear, release the grief.

ELIZABETH: That moron ruined my life while he was alive and
              now he's screwing me up after his own fucking death.

MARGE: Just let the tears flow.

IAN: How is it that women can talk so much without ever
              hearing each other?

ELIZABETH: Shut up! It's not as though you ever listened to me.

IAN: I did at first. I just started tuning you out after a while.

ELIZABETH: Well, maybe if you had paid attention once in a while
              we wouldn't have had such issues, and you wouldn't
              have gotten involved with that tart.

IAN: Cindy was not a tart. She was a perfectly nice woman.

MARGE: Lizzie? I get the feeling that you're not giving me your
              full attention.

IAN: Cindy would never have buried me in this god-awful
              suit.

ELIZABETH: Sorry, Aunt Marge. I'm just a little…preoccupied right
              now.

IAN: I look like a used car salesman from the seventies.

ELIZABETH: Your tailor made it for you.

IAN: I meant to fire him, but then I died.

MARGE: Your grief is about to spill over, isn't it?

ELIZABETH: Yes. Yes it is. Would you be wonderful and go find me
              some Kleenex?

MARGE: I keep this handy-dandy packet right here in my
              purse. (She rummages in her enormous handbag.)

ELIZABETH: Oh, wait. I forgot…I'm allergic to Kleenex.

MARGE: Allergic to Kleenex?

IAN: Allergic to Kleenex?

ELIZABETH: Yes. Allergic. Exactly. All those little…dust…bits… they get in my nose and fly around.

IAN: Lizzie, why don't you just ask for some privacy?

ELIZABETH: As if that ever worked with Aunt Marge.

MARGE: OK, dear. I'm going to get you a hanky. A great big hanky for my poor little mourning girl. Are you going to be alright if I leave you here?

ELIZABETH: I think I can manage.

MARGE: Alright. Just you sit tight. Aunt Margie is going to be right back. OK?

ELIZABETH: OK.

MARGE: OK. *(She exits.)*

IAN: OK.

ELIZABETH: Shut up! You just shut up!

IAN: She's going to be back you know. You've bought yourself maybe five minutes of peace.

ELIZABETH: Peace? You think talking to you is peace? You…you… backstabbing…stubborn…dead…man!

IAN: Oh, let me rest in peace.

ELIZABETH: You let me rest in peace!

IAN: I'm just trying to be dead, here.

ELIZABETH: Look. I don't want to talk to you. Go away. Fly off on little wings…plummet into hell…go…reincarnate into a butterfly. Which I will then squish.

IAN: Hey, I don't control this thing. Believe me, I'd much rather be out of here.

ELIZABETH: Get out of my head, OK? Stop. Talking. We are going to say goodbye now. You are going to stop bothering me. I am not going to think about you any more. I have made my peace. Goodbye. Namaste. Au revoir. Fuck off.

IAN: Fine. *(He lies back down.)*

ELIZABETH: Fine. *(Silence…)* Ian? *(No response.)* Ian? Ian, are you gone? Iaaaan… He's gone. He's out of my head. He's—

IAN: *(Popping up suddenly.)* BOO!

ELIZABETH: AAH! Ian! No! Go away! I made peace with you. Now you need to leave me alone. Go to the light, Ian. Go to the liiight…

IAN: There isn't one, Lizzie.

ELIZABETH: Ian! Go to the fucking light!

IAN: That's not how it works.

ELIZABETH: Not how it works? What, you die once and suddenly you're an expert?

IAN: I've seen a lot of movies, OK? You can't just tell me to fuck off and that's the end of it.

ELIZABETH: I just want you to be dead! Why is this such an issue? Everyone else's dead husbands stay dead.

IAN: *(Flustered with anger.)* If everyone else's dead husband jumped off a bridge, would you…

ELIZABETH: What?

IAN: There really was no way to finish that sentence.

ELIZABETH: *(The wind has gone out of her sails just a little.)* I hate you, Ian.

IAN: I know.

ELIZABETH: I didn't always, but I do now.

IAN: I know.

ELIZABETH: How could you do that to me? How could you?

IAN: "How"?

ELIZABETH: How?

IAN: How?!

ELIZABETH: Yes, how, that's what I'm asking you, how could you
                do this to me?

IAN: I can't believe this.

ELIZABETH: What?

IAN: This! This! Yeah, Lizzie, I fucked up, but you honestly
                have no idea how this came around?

ELIZABETH: No, I don't.

IAN: Unbelievable. We split up, I have a fling, I become
                the devil, and all of the shit you put me through just
                washes away.

ELIZABETH: "What I put you through?" Do you know how many
                guys would KILL to be with me? Do you know how
                many?

IAN: I don't give a shit.

ELIZABETH: Tons! And I never even looked at another man from
                the day I said my vows, but we go through a little
                choppy water and it's "Oh, comfort me, Cindy!"

IAN: Of course you never looked at another man, you've
                had a headache for the better half of two years!

ELIZABETH: Die, Ian! Die, die die! *(IAN falls over into the coffin.)*
                Oh, really funny, sweetie. I'm not falling for it this
                time. *(No response.)* Ian, I can feel you're still there.
                (N/R.) Fine. Just be dead. Because we both know that
                I didn't put you through anything and this whole
                thing is your fault. *(N/R.)* Ian? Ian, I have to tell you

something. *(N/R.)* Fine, then you'll never know what it is. *(N/R.)* I'm glad you're gone, you know. I don't need you around. *(N/R.)* Ian, stop fucking around, I know you're still there! *(N/R.)* Ian, I'm pregnant.

IAN: *(Popping up.)* WHAT?

ELIZABETH: I knew it, you rat-bastard!

              The next dozen lines or so overlap.

IAN: You're pregnant?!

ELIZABETH: You asshole, stop doing that to me!

IAN: PREGNANT?!

ELIZABETH: I am going to KILL YOU.

IAN: How could you not tell me?!

ELIZABETH: I am going to kill you very dead. Where's a shovel?

IAN: PREGNANT? You're PREGNANT?

ELIZABETH: No, I'm not pregnant, you scum-sucking dirtbag.

IAN: You're pregnant and you wait until after I'm dead to tell me?

ELIZABETH: Ian!

IAN: Jesus Christ, Lizzie, how long have you known I was going to be a dad?

ELIZABETH: Ian. I'm not pregnant.

IAN: What?

ELIZABETH: I. Am not. Pregnant.

IAN: Why the fuck did you say you were, then?

ELIZABETH: To get you to stop playing dead…ish.

IAN: Jesus. Wait, you're sure you're not pregnant?

ELIZABETH: Yes.

IAN: Jesus. You're sure?

ELIZABETH: Ian, you have to have sex to get pregnant, even by accident.

IAN: We had sex.

ELIZABETH: No one gets pregnant from that amount of sex. The sperm gets sluggish.

IAN: There are sixteen-year-old girls who get pregnant from that amount of sex. Though I suppose they weren't lying to their husbands about being on the Pill.

ELIZABETH: I didn't lie to you.

IAN: When you agree to try for kids and secretly take the Pill, that's called lying.

ELIZABETH: Don't try to blame our problems on me, you're the one with the—

IAN: Former flying nun, yeah, and I'm sorry.

ELIZABETH: No you're not.

IAN: Yes I am. I'm sorry.

ELIZABETH: Fuck off, Ian.

IAN: Lizzie, I'm sorry, alright, I truly am. I was drunk, I was angry, I wasn't thinking. But you kicked me out.

ELIZABETH: You deserved it.

IAN: Because I got angry and left the house briefly after finding out you'd been lying for a year? What about counseling or something?

ELIZABETH: You could never handle counseling! Not in a million years! And do you know why?

IAN: I'm sure you're about to tell me!

ELIZABETH: Because you are incapable of listening.

IAN: You're incapable of telling the truth, why would I listen to your lies? "Sure Ian, let's try for kids while I stay on the Pill!"

ELIZABETH: You would never have listened to me anyway! Look at this! Has a heart attack, bites it, and still yelling at me!

IAN: Drop dead!

ELIZABETH: Get a life! (Silence...)

IAN: I really wanted kids.

ELIZABETH: Yes, we know Ian, I know, everybody knows that you wanted kids, but guess what, I didn't.

IAN: Well, you could have just told me.

ELIZABETH: No, I couldn't.

IAN: Yes, you could!

ELIZABETH: No, I couldn't. I wanted to. But every time it came up, it was all, "Oh, you'll be such a great mom, I'm so excited, I want kids, I'm an asshole, blah blah blah..."

IAN: I don't remember adding that last part.

ELIZABETH: And I figured, you know...you would hate me if I said "no."

IAN: ·   I wouldn't have hated you.

ELIZABETH: Well, you moved on pretty quick to not loving me.

IAN: After I found out that you had been lying to me for a year!

ELIZABETH: You didn't have to walk out on me!

IAN: You didn't have to throw my stuff all over the front lawn!

ELIZABETH: You didn't have to take that to mean that we were splitting up!

IAN: You left a note on the door! "Ian. We need some time apart. I get the TV. Signed, Elizabeth." And you screened all of my calls. I must have left a hundred messages.

ELIZABETH: I tried calling you back, but you were too busy to talk to me! I just called to discuss things, but oh no, you were too busy with your floozy secretary.

IAN: You didn't call to discuss things, you called to scream about Cindy.

ELIZABETH: Yeah, the first time I did. The second time I called asking to talk things over. And you never called me back. I humiliated myself! I called to work things out and you never called me back, you horrible person!

IAN: I couldn't call you back.

ELIZABETH: Yeah, because your misogynistic pride got in the way.

IAN: No, because I died.

ELIZABETH: Oh, always an excuse.

IAN: Lizzie, I'm not going to apologize for having a heart attack before I got your message.

ELIZABETH: Fine. But at least apologize for sleeping with your secretary.

IAN: For God's sake, Lizzie, I already did.

ELIZABETH: Did you?

IAN: Yes! But if it makes you happy, I'm sorry. I'm very sorry, and I wish I had waited for things to calm down before I did such a stupid thing. I didn't have feelings for her, you know.

ELIZABETH: None?

IAN: None at all.

ELIZABETH: Good.

IAN: And...?

ELIZABETH: And what?

IAN: And, "Well, Ian, I'm really sorry about lying to you and throwing your stuff on the lawn and stealing your brand new 50-inch flat-panel Panasonic."

ELIZABETH: Yeah.

IAN: Yeah, what?

ELIZABETH: Yeah, I'm sorry I lied and kept your stupid TV.

IAN: Good.

ELIZABETH: Good. *(Silence.)* ...So, all these movies...what do they say happens now?

IAN: Well, you've made your peace, I've made my peace... so right about now I should float off.

ELIZABETH: Right. Bye, Ian.

IAN: Bye, Lizzie. *(He lies back down. Nothing happens. He lifts one arm out of the coffin. Nothing. He lifts the other arm. He looks very stupid. Nothing. He pokes his head up.)* Any minute now. *(He settles back down.)*

ELIZABETH: Ian?

IAN: Hmm?

ELIZABETH: Did I kill you?

IAN: *(Sitting up.)* What?

ELIZABETH: Is it my fault you died?

IAN: Don't be so melodramatic.

ELIZABETH: I'm serious. *(She looks at him.)* Did all of that fighting...

all the time, me kicking you out, all that…stress… stress causes heart attacks, I've read that before.

IAN: Lizzie, you didn't kill me.

ELIZABETH: Are you sure?

IAN: Yeah. *(He reaches to touch her but can't. She is staring off into the distance and doesn't even notice. A long pause. He settles back down.)*

ELIZABETH: Are you really sure? God, I hope not. *(A long pause.)* I loved you. *(Beat.)* Ian? Ian?

                Enter AUNT MARGE.

ELIZABETH: Ian?

MARGE: I'm back dear. Here's your hanky. *(ELIZABETH takes it, almost in shock.)* Honestly, does no one carry hankies any more? I finally found one, needless to say, but you don't want to know where. My poor dear. You're in so much pain.

ELIZABETH: Ian, you bastard, you can't leave me here now.

MARGE: It's OK, dear.

ELIZABETH: He's gone.

MARGE: I know, dear. Strange when it starts to set in, isn't it?

ELIZABETH: He's gone, I can't feel him any more, he's gone… *(She shakes herself.)* I don't want to stay here any more.

MARGE: But dear, they'll come to bury him soon!

ELIZABETH: I've been waiting for hours, I'm not waiting any more.

MARGE: Oh. OK then. I suppose I'll come with you.

ELIZABETH: Thanks Aunt Marge.

MARGE: They're running out of appetizers up there anyhow. *(She picks up a handful of dirt and dumps it into the coffin.)*

Ashes to ashes. *(She exits.)*

ELIZABETH: *(Picking up a handful of dirt and pouring it in.)* Dust to
dust.

> *She stares for a moment and then follows AUNT
> MARGE out. Brief pause before IAN throws the dirt
> back out again. Lights down.*

> *The End.*

Penance

Bailey MacLeod

"This play won the Cora McKenzie Award for First Place in our tenth anniversary year, 2010. It raised a lot of interesting questions about life, and being human—and maybe even answered a few. It's a story of redemption that connected with the audience in a big way." —A.K.

> *It is the middle of the night in a central city park. GERARD is sleeping on the ground. WARDEN, SUSAN and BRITTANY are in the background, they take turns mimicking GERARD and the PARK WARDEN's actions. He is in a hospital gown the background noise of a hospital fills the air.*

PARK
WARDEN: Hey buddy! What! You don't hear me? Wake up! You need to leave or I am going to call an ambulance, though I would hate to waste their time with a worthless piece of scum like you. Well, are you going to wake up?

GERARD: It's not like they are going to do anything, besides giving me a nicer place to sleep. I guess you wouldn't understand. Anyways, it's not like you have had to sleep on a dilapidated bench before.

> *PARK WARDEN stops and looks anxious.*

> *GERARD mocking.*

Oh wait, you have?! The man on his power trip has slept on a bench? Oh, to what did you owe such a pleasure? You think someone such as yourself would be above a thing like that. Because you have what?

> *PARK WARDEN tries to interrupt but GERARD positions his finger over his mouth.*

A blue collar, barely working class job. I thought benches were only for common vagrants like myself. Who knew they were also handy for a man of your esteem.

> *GERARD bows.*

PARK
WARDEN: Why don't you knock it off right now!

GERARD: Oh boo, I was hoping for something much more stereotypical alpha male. Though I guess that would require you to comprehend what I am saying. Let's try this, one more time, shall we? *(Aside.)* Because god only knows how hard it is to belittle someone who can't understand you.

> *Speaking in an elongated tone.*

I think you are a moron. Get it?

PARK
WARDEN: I'm going to give you, to the count'a ten, before I pummel you!

GERARD: In that case, I might as well leave before you hurt yourself, it should give you some time to work out those mommy issues you have.

> *PARK WARDEN grabs GERARD by his coat and throws him out of the park.*

Oh, how nice it is to be touched by a strong man like yourself.

> *GERARD turns and winks at the park warden. The PARK WARDEN turns and leaves. GERARD begins to sob on a bus stop bench directly outside of the park. Lights dim hospital sound track begins to play.*

Oh God, I think I am coming down, but that would mean that I have something or somewhere to come down from. The one good thing about never living up to your full potential is that there is always a lot to dream about. My old friends at least have families to pass the burden onto. The closest I have ever come to a family is just a name, Callahan. It was my mother's last name since she never wed or even bothered to find out who my father was, but we must not speak ill of the dead, God rest her soul. Having no family or any real connections I've always thought about my funeral; who would make the arrangements, who would come to mourn my passing? Some say that a funeral is the final tying of strings in the ball of yarn that is our lives; I disagree with the statement but I do agree that dying is the final tying of strings. The fact that our lives are a ball of yarn is completely absurd. Could they pick a more useless object as a metaphor for our lives? Sure yarn brings joy to kittens and old women with arthritis. At the end of the day kittens become tired of yarn and move onto better forms of escape such as cat nip and as for the old women, who cares? She is bound to die soon anyways. The funny thing is, we all die, maybe it isn't so funny perhaps more tragic than anything. Live alone, die alone it's bound to be my life. But…the truth is, we all die, so I will never really be doing it alone. I once read that one hundred and seven people die every minute, which gives me a pretty large chance that someone will die on my minute.

A child, BRITTANY, comes and sits beside GERARD.

BRITTANY: Are you going to stop crying soon Mister? Because this is my bus stop and my mother told me to wait here and nowhere else and you see, I wouldn't want to sit near you for the simple fact it may be contagious.

GERARD: Contagious?

BRITTANY: Yes, my mother always told me bad moods are contagious and you see today is my first day at a new school so I really can't have that on my shoulders.

GERARD: Oh yes how dare I not think of that. Well I think you are safe, all of my tears are gone for now.

BRITTANY: Well it's a good thing because my mother says it can lead to dehydration, and dehydration is a common contributor to headaches.

GERARD: What is your name?

BRITTANY: I'm afraid I can't tell you, my mother told me, never talk to strangers.

GERARD: Your mother sounds like a wise woman.

BRITTANY: May I ask, why you're so sad?

GERARD: I guess I've just been down on my luck, but that's how she goes kid.

BRITTANY: Did you know a pessimistic viewpoint makes you four times more likely to catch the common cold.

GERARD: Let me guess another fact from your mother?

BRITTANY: Nope, I saw it on a public service announcement but she would probably endorse it though. I would appreciate it if you kept that between me and you. I would get in a heap of trouble if she found out that I snuck in and was watching TV; she might even kick me out of the house. Then I would get kicked out of school, and my bright future would be thrown down the drain and I would become a hom— *(BRITTANY hesitates and remembers who he is talking to.)* I mean, I'd become hopeless.

GERARD: Don't worry, the last thing I need after me is an angry mother. Women are always trouble.

             BRITTANY glares at GERARD, GERARD appears unchanged by the reaction. Some time passes and BRITTANY starts to fidget.

BRITTANY: I just can't wait to be older so I can spread my wings and carpe diem, although, I'm not really positive what that means. I see it on travel ads so I think carpe diem is somewhere that I am interested in visiting.

GERARD: It's not as great as it's chalked up to be. It's hard to seize the day when tomorrow is always looming over your shoulder.

BRITTANY: My travel choices are none of your business, Mister.

GERARD: You just want to feel the sun on your skin? Because myself, I would kill for a little sun on my skin.

BRITTANY: I'd rather not, ultraviolet radiation can lead to melanoma which can be life shattering.

GERARD: What do you think melanoma is?

BRITTANY: I'm not really sure about that either but I don't want to find out; that's why, I spend all the time I can, inside.

GERARD: I feel bad for you kid, for the simple fact that you're what, ten years old?

BRITTANY: Eleven.

GERARD: That's beside the point, you have eleven years under your belt and you're already willing to wait your life away. Tomorrow will always come, but today is the foundation for tomorrow. If you don't make the best of it now, you may never get to visit carpe diem like you said you wanted to.

BRITTANY: I could say the same for you, Mister.

GERARD: My name is Gerard.

BRITTANY: Yeah whatever, my mother told me, never talk to strangers. The point is I'm not the one sitting here moping on this bus bench with nowhere to go. I may not have lived a lot like you, but I have many years to strategically plot out my life goals and plan my RRSP's.

GERARD: I can tell you are a very intelligent girl, intelligence is something that you will need to work your way through life, and the thing that is most important is that you're still a kid. You will learn some day, that it is not only the large things but also the simple pleasures in life that are passing you by. You know this whole conversation, I haven't seen you smile! Go out and play in the sun, smile and enjoy everything that life and freedom have to offer.

BRITTANY: I must go catch my bus or I won't be able to escape the scolding that I can foresee, if I miss it.

GERARD: Youth is something that passes us all by. Some of us embrace it with everything we have and others let it slip by without taking the chance to mould anything great out of it. If I could start over again, I guess my youth is where I would begin, my teen years actually. As much as people like to tell you that one through ten are the years that form your personality and the person that you will become, I disagree. The teen years, are the years when you taste your first sense of rebellion, your first true hurt, and generally your first love outside of your family. Those three things are the backbone to every successful life because no other time will you feel the higher highs or the lower lows. Every now and then, I still feel youth coursing through my veins and it is always: adrenaline with rebellion, anger with hurt and ache with love. Those three feelings are something that we can never truly master and that is why it takes us back to the turbulent times of being young; when we thought we had a chance of one day getting over these feelings.

Lights dim, hospital back round noise begins to play again. GERARD is still in the hospital gown.

GERARD moves from his perch at the bus stop to sit underneath the tree due to the sweltering mid day heat. The park is not crowded due to the heat, but there are a couple passers by. A woman walks past GERARD, spilling her books on him.

SUSAN: Oh sorry! I didn't mean to wake you.

> *GERARD picks up the celebrity gossip magazine that fell on him and passes it to SUSAN.*

Oh thank you.

GERARD: You know it's not as glamorous as they make it out to be.

SUSAN: It never is, it seems like every story the media gets their hands on gets so manipulated that there is absolutely no comparison between the original story and the one that gets mass produced and spit shined, for all to see, but it doesn't make it any less entertaining.

GERARD: It's their job to sell the magazine, not to tell the truth. You would have to be delusional to buy into that.

SUSAN: Well it's a good thing that I don't isn't it?

GERARD: Then why did you buy the magazine? Because, no sane person would spend $3.75 just to mock something in private and pick out the fallacies.

SUSAN: Although I hate almost everything about the paper, I am a sucker for Hollywood gossip and the idea of the "perfect life."

GERARD: There is no such thing as the perfect life, only the illusion of one and I think I can be a testament to that.

SUSAN: I guess it's just an escape, to look at someone else's life that is far worse than mine. It just makes you feel grateful for everything that you have, you know?

> *GERARD scowls.*

GERARD: I don't think I share the same kind of joy that you do. To seek happiness from others misery is not true happiness, you are just falling for the exact thing the media wants you to. You pointed out the fact that the media manipulates but see nothing wrong with the way it is toying with your emotions?

> *SUSAN scowls.*

SUSAN: .   I'm not the only one who buys into it.

GERARD: I am not saying that you are, but before you go on an
             elitist spiel then I suggest you have something to back
             it up with or it makes you one hell of an easy target.

SUSAN: I have to go.

GERARD: What, can't take a friendly rousing?

SUSAN: No, it's just that I don't wish to take one from someone
             of your position.

GERARD: And what position might that be?

SUSAN: Uhh

GERARD: Homeless? Well yes, I may be lacking of physical
             shelter, but I view myself as being quite wealthy.

                     SUSAN sarcastic.

SUSAN: Let me guess, emotional wealth?

GERARD: Oh you are very clever, but that was long ago.

SUSAN: Might I ask what happened?

GERARD: Oh isn't that kind of you, pretending to be interested
             in me! It wasn't my choice. I was in the army and
             my best friend was hurt by my side and there was
             nothing I could do about it. Everyday, I wish I could
             have the chance to relive that moment and re-think
             my decisions. I must stop wishing because that day
             will never come.

SUSAN: Oh, I am sorry to hear about that.

GERARD: No you're not and you shouldn't be. We all have our
             own battles and they should not burden others.

SUSAN: I guess I'm not, but it doesn't mean that I can't feel
             compassion for others.

GERARD: How about compassion for those in the public eye?

SUSAN: They chose that life and the attention that goes with it.

GERARD: I agree, they chose the attention but not the scrutiny that comes along with every single action they make. We all make mistakes but we should be confronting ourselves without the world looking in on us like we live in a fish bowl. All I am saying is that they are people much like any other and we have no right to criticize or take emotional happiness from their downfalls. If you would like to judge, at least wait until you have been formally introduced. Hello, my name is Gerard.

SUSAN: My name is Susan.

GERARD: Well it's a pleasure Susan, now where is the judgment?

            SUSAN sits silently and uncomfortably.

SUSAN: You have no right to put me on the spot like this.

GERARD: And why not? Is this not what you have been asking for the whole time? Take a cheap shot at me, its not like they all aren't obvious. You don't even have the respect to give me a "When was the last time you showered?" I really thought more of you.

SUSAN: Now you're judging me?

GERARD: Well yes, we have been formally introduced after all.

SUSAN: Well excuse me but one cannot be on top of their mental game whilst being forced into a conversation.

GERARD: No one can be forced into a conversation; must I remind you, that you have been replying to everything I am saying? Though with such thoughtless replies it hasn't been much of a conversation anyways.

SUSAN: *(Says haughtily.)* —Maybe I am not telling you what I think about you because you are not worthy of my opinion, if you could even understand me that is.

GERARD: Finally, something genuine coming out of your mouth, I am quite surprised! People tend to tell the truth when you make them angry because once the barriers are down, they lose all regard for the other's well being.

SUSAN: Is this all some game to you?

GERARD: No, I would never play with someones emotions. Though I will do whatever I have to, to get an honest conversation.

SUSAN: Well fine, you have me, what do you want?

GERARD: I want to know why you are so caught up in the lives of others?

SUSAN: I am a nurse, it does not make interpersonal relationships easy. I work in the ICU and over the years I've had to thicken my skin so my work doesn't follow me home.

GERARD: But it still does, doesn't it?

SUSAN: Yes, I am not some heartless bitch. You can't watch people die every day and not be impacted in some way. Hence the magazines, seeing their lives allows me to live vicariously through the rollercoaster of human emotion without the attachment.

GERARD: Are you single?

SUSAN: Great, and now I have a homeless guy, in a park, taking a swipe at me!

GERARD: Don't flatter yourself.

SUSAN: You think you are going to get me to tell you by insulting me, I hardly think so.

             Silence. SUSAN begins to fidget.

             Fine, I'm single.

GERARD: I know.

SUSAN becomes enraged at the comment.

SUSAN: Its not like it's always been this way! We were engaged.

GERARD: What happened?

SUSAN: He was on his way to work and was involved in a horrific car crash... He probably could have made it if the hospital wasn't backed up. I was on shift but I had no idea.

Silence.

For Christ sake, would you just say something!

GERARD: Losing a loved one can be a horrible travesty but I bet you work harder than anyone else at that hospital now.

SUSAN stands up and begins to yell.

SUSAN: I BET YOU WORK HARD?

GERARD: Well yes, it must give you motivation.

SUSAN defeated.

SUSAN: You can't even give me a half hearted, I'm sorry for your loss.

GERARD: I am sure you have heard it all before and a simple condolence from the homeless guy in the park is not going to change anything. It's over and has been for a while, I'm guessing.

SUSAN: Yes, but it doesn't make a difference being in the same building on shift knowing you could have done something, anything, and to just let that slip through your fingers it's impossible to forget.

GERARD: Inner demons have a way of making you stronger, if you don't let them take you over completely. Forgiving yourself cannot be forced.

SUSAN gives GERARD a blank stare.

Well you're still here aren't you! All you really want from this is a small bit of real human interaction where you won't have to hold the other persons hand through it. Or have I got you all wrong?

SUSAN: I don't know.

GERARD: You will someday, that's the beauty of it. You have all the time that the world allows to make things right, and sometimes, it does get cut shorter than you would like, but things have a way of tying themselves up in the end.

SUSAN: I don't want to talk about myself anymore.

GERARD: What would you prefer, the weather, sports or geographical politics?

SUSAN: Tell me about your friend.

GERARD: He died a long time ago so there is no use in worrying about it now.

SUSAN: You're avoiding me. What happened to him?

GERARD: Like you, I also lost someone I loved, but it was at my own hand. I have never forgiven myself for it.

           Silence.

           You can stop running over scenarios in your head to come up with reasons to leave; you are not at risk, I didn't kill him, but I led him to his death. He was in my platoon and I made the order to move out. He was such a loyal friend that he took my word and now look where he is for it.

SUSAN: He was sent to my hospital. If I had been on the floor when he came in, he may still be here today.

GERARD: Blame must be laid in a situation like that, I made the call and his life was lost. The worst part is I got an honourable discharge. Honourable would be the word that least described my actions, cowardice is more accurate.

SUSAN: You can't blame yourself for that.

GERARD: When I got home I gave all of the money I had to his family, and every time I work an odd job I send the money to them. He had three daughters. That's why I am here on the streets, any money I make goes to his family as a form of penance. It is the only way I can sleep at night. We all have to do things to find peace. The hard part isn't living on the streets; it is the fact that it will never be enough.

SUSAN: Gerard, you must take your own advice, you have helped me and now it is time to help yourself. Is there anything I could do for you?

GERARD: No

              SUSAN now pleading.

SUSAN: Something tells me there is something I can do. Anything, I'll do it.

GERARD: There is nothing you can do for me, though there is something that you can do for yourself. As you said, life is a rollercoaster and if you keep protecting yourself from emotions you may never feel the lows but you will also miss out on the most beautiful part of life, and that is the highs. We all can experience the middle, but it takes someone who is truly open to everything that life has to offer to experience the rest. If you stop hiding behind celebrities you will feel the true range of human emotion that you lost with the passing of your fiancé. You may never see me again but you will have to live the rest of your life with your actions so please make them purposeful. Now please go and enjoy the rest of the sunshine.

SUSAN: Thank you, but I really must urge you to take your own advice.

              SUSAN exits.

GERARD: I guess I have always been a hypocrite. It's always easier to deal with other people's problems; it's a lot less personal. I guess that's why I am so hung up on the idea of my funeral, because it is the first time that my problems will be transferred onto someone else. My whole life, I have dealt with handling my problems on my own terms. I wonder what I will warrant in the after life? There's one thing that will always stand out, it's the idea of redemption I don't know if I've always been a believer but I think my time for penance is finally up.

Scene opens in an emergency room. GERARD is lying on the table with massive injuries to his abdomen; he is covered in blood and hardly recognizable. He is accompanied by A nurse, SUSAN, and a DOCTOR.

SUSAN: Sir what's your name? Sir? Can you hear? WAKE UP SIR!

SUSAN checks for pupil dilation. GERARD is still unresponsive. SUSAN hands the DOCTOR a spread sheet.

DOCTOR: What do we have?

SUSAN: A male in his mid- to late thirties with severe trauma to his abdominal cavity with deep lacerations on his face and arms.

DOCTOR: What happened?

DOCTOR and SUSAN both continue to work over GERARD.

SUSAN: He was struck by a bus. Sir are you awake? Can you hear me?

DOCTOR: It was bound to happen sooner or latter, the bum was probably drunk.

SUSAN: He was pushing a child out of the way.

Both continue to work silently. Eventually. GERARD

begins to show signs of consciousness. DOCTOR exits.

SUSAN: What's your name? Can you tell me where you are?

BRITTANY enters.

You were hit by a bus trying to push a young girl out of the way, you're a hero.

BRITTANY: Hello sir, how are you?

GERARD: I thought your mother told you to never talk to strangers?

BRITTANY: Who cares about my mother, plus someone who almost died for you hardly counts as a stranger.

GERARD: Yes, plus you wouldn't want to catch what I have.

BRITTANY: Internal bleeding isn't contagious.

GERARD: Oh right, that was only bad moods.

BRITTANY: I'm Brittany.

BRITTANY and GERARD shake hands.

GERARD: Sergeant Gerard Callahan.

BRITTANY: Are you going to be alright?

GERARD: I think I'll be just fine.

The End.

Biographies of Contributors

LAUREN PARSONS: Lauren is a graduate of Kelvin High School and studied Theatre and Film at the University of Winnipeg. She currently lives in Winnipeg and is studying Creative Communications at Red River College.

COLIN SHELTON: Colin grew up in the various Kildonans of north Winnipeg, before moving to Seattle for graduate school. He currently teaches Greek and Latin literature at Memorial University of Newfoundland, in St. John's.

CORA MCKENZIE: Cora was an aspiring writer from Portage la Prairie, Manitoba. Her mother once told MAP that it had been Cora's dream to be published one day.

HANNAH PRODAN: Hannah was raised in Brandon, Manitoba and is currently attending university with hopes of one day receiving her PHD in Indigenous Studies. Although she has always had a love for writing, *Kaddy* was her first venture into playwriting.

DEVON FORD: Devon plays hockey for the Gladstone Lakers, and is studying Arts at Brandon University. He plans to go into Education.

DYLAN GYLES: Dylan writes stage plays, screenplays, and short stories of both the fiction and science fiction variety. He currently resides in Vancouver and is an avid supporter of the reading of books and the watching of *Star Wars*.

ROCHELLE FOUREE: Rocki, in her own words, says "I grew up thinking that I was never going to escape the dysfunctional cycle my family was living under. It wasn't until I got to know God on a much personal level that I finally realized that he does not promise us a problem free life. He does however, offer us the power and the ability through his grace, to change our hearts which can ultimately bring us peace and happiness. It is only because of God that I was able to really

"Let Go" of my past and enjoy my future, and I really couldn't have done this without him."

MARIA FUNK: From a young age Maria has been very passionate about reading and writing, and, once she was introduced to the theatre, she expanded her repertoire to scripts and monologues. She believes that the characters, no matter the medium, should always be the vehicles for telling the story.

JESSY ARDERN: Jessy is a student of procrastination at the University of Winnipeg. She was a co-winner (with Ariel Levine) of the Harry Rintoul Award for Best New Manitoba Play at the Winnipeg Fringe Festival this year (2011).

BAILEY MACLEOD: Bailey is an aspiring writer who originally hails from Calgary, Alberta (but moved to Manitoba). She is currently studying at the University of Toronto.

ANGUS KOHM: Angus is a playwright and musician who is probably best known for his musical comedy *Sorority Girls Slumber Party Massacre: The Musical*. He created the Manitoba High School Playwriting Competition as a one-time fundraiser in 2001, and has been producing it every year since. Learn more at: anguskohm.com

RORY RUNNELLS: Rory has been the Artistic Director of the Manitoba Association of Playwrights since 1983.

The Official Results from the First Ten Years of the Scirocco Drama Manitoba High School Playwriting Competition

2001

1st Place

The Old Lie by Katherine Coerdt, Christelle Manaigre, and Cherie Perrier, Collége Lorette Collegiate, Lorette

2nd Place

The Eagle Princess by Amanda Barbeau, Frontier Collegiate, Cranberry-Portage

3rd Place

Mixed Up Fairy Tales by Deborah Vanbeek, Deborah VanderLinde, and Pamela Shpak, Immanuel Christian School, Winnipeg

Honourable Mentions

An Old Man's Face by Cole Robson-Hyska, Dakota Collegiate, Winnipeg

He Can't Be by Odessa Bashuk-Riechel, Garden City Collegiate, Winnipeg

2002

1st Place

An Ordinary Girl by Lauren Parsons, Kelvin High School, Winnipeg

2nd Place

In Wonderland by Christine Kampen, Westgate Mennonite Collegiate, Winnipeg

3rd Place

On the Road by Colin Shelton, Westgate Mennonite Collegiate, Winnipeg

Honourable Mentions

Twist of Fate by Cole Robson-Hyska, Dakota Collegiate, Winnipeg

Waves on the Shore by Marieke Breakey, Westwood Collegiate, Winnipeg

2003

1st Place

.COM by Cora McKenzie, Portage Collegiate, Portage la Prairie

2nd Place

A Disconnection by Ashley Sy and Katherine Vong, Kelvin High School, Winnipeg

3rd Place

Harlot, Queen of Denmark by Craig Haas, Westwood Collegiate, Winnipeg

Honourable Mentions

It's Simple by Jenna Tichon, Westwood Collegiate, Winnipeg

Escape by David Barkman, Westwood Collegiate, Winnipeg

2004

1st Place

Virgin Falls by Alyssa Stefanson, Westwood Collegiate, Winnipeg

2nd Place

Kaddy by Hannah Prodan, Crocus Plains Regional Secondary School, Brandon

3rd Place

The Case of the White Truffle by Grace Bowness, Collége Churchill, Winnipeg

Honourable Mentions

Faces Time-Lapsed by Josh Grummett, John Taylor Collegiate, Winnipeg

New Order by Michelle Bigold, St. James Collegiate, Winnipeg

2005

1st Place

Take It by Dylan Gyles, Kelvin High School, Winnipeg

2nd Place

Hockey Life in Canada by Devon Ford, Portage Collegiate, Portage la Prairie

3rd Place

A Play by Joseph Black by Conrad Sweatman, Kelvin High School, Winnipeg

Honourable Mentions:

The Village of Life by Grace Bowness, College Churchill, Winnipeg

The Right Thing To Do by Theresa McIver, Westwood Collegiate, Winnipeg

2006

1st Place

Think, Then Speak by Dylan Gyles, Kelvin High School, Winnipeg

2nd Place

Eckvile by Joseph Tritt, University of Winnipeg Collegiate, Winnipeg

3rd Place

Letting Go by Rochelle Fourre, Tec Voc High School, Winnipeg

Honourable Mentions

Rubber Boots and Bamboo Shoots by Kaitlyn McDermid, Portage Collegiate, Portage la Prairie

Missing Maureen by Jessy Ardern, Vincent Massey Collegiate, Winnipeg

2007

Cora McKenzie Award for First Place

45 Reasons Why I Hate the World by Dylan Gyles, Kelvin High School, Winnipeg

Second Place

In The Hot Seat by Kaitlyn McDermid, Portage Collegiate, Portage la Prairie

Third Place

Perspective by Maria Funk, Tec Voc High School, Winnipeg

Honourable Mentions

I'll Be Seeing You by Ashley Alberg, West Kildonan Collegiate, Winnipeg

Colour of Love by Chanelle Holder, Vincent Massey Collegiate, Winnipeg

2008

Cora McKenzie Award for First Place:

I Dream of Jimmy by Ashley Alberg, West Kildonan Collegiate, Winnipeg

Second Place

The Love Triangle by K.R. Byggdin, Niverville Collegiate, Niverville

Third Place

Death (And Other Small Issues of Communication) by Jessy Ardern, Vincent Massey Collegiate, Winnipeg

Honourable Mentions

Don't Forget About Us by Kris Longmuir, Tec Voc High School, Winnipeg

Caroline by Cherrel Holder, Vincent Massey Collegiate, Winnipeg

2009

Cora McKenzie Award for First Place
Dirty Rotten Un Loved Zombie: The Musical by Shelby Thevenot and Aaron McAuley, Portage Collegiate, Portage la Prairie

Second Place
Tooth Fairies: A Night In The Life by Hannia Curi, Vincent Massey Collegiate, Winnipeg

Third Place
The Voice by Corinne M. Coutts, University of Winnipeg Collegiate, Winnipeg

Honourable Mentions
The Truth by Dustin Monkman, Tec Voc High School, Winnipeg

The Guilty Conscience of a Teenage Mind by Nathan Costa, Tec Voc High School, Winnipeg

2010

Cora McKenzie Award for First Place
Penance by Bailey MacLeod , University of Winnipeg Collegiate, Winnipeg

Second Place
Never Turn Back by Caitlin Gannon, Tec Voc High School, Winnipeg

Third Place
How Did I Die? by Kaylyn Kalupar, Collége St. Norbert Collegiate, St. Norbert

Honourable Mentions
Lost Soul by Nathan Hill, Portage Collegiate, Portage la Prairie

Possessed By Magic by Jessica Gomes, Nelson McIntyre Collegiate, Winnipeg